MILLENNIUM

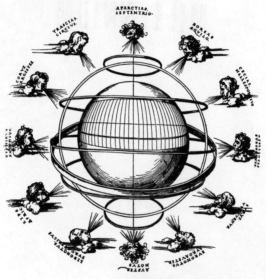

JACQUES ATTALI

MILLENNIUM

Winners and Losers in
the Coming World Order

TRANSLATED
FROM THE FRENCH BY
LEILA CONNERS
AND NATHAN GARDELS

TIMES BOOKS

Library of Congress Cataloging-in-Publication Data

Attali, Jacques.
[Lignes d'horizons. English]
Millennium: winners and losers in the coming world order /
Jacques Attali; translated from the French by Leila Conners
and Nathan Gardels.—1st ed.
p.   cm.
ISBN 0–8129–2088–0 (pbk.)
1. World politics—1989– 2. Twenty-first century–Forecasts.
I. Title.
D860.A88   1991
303.49′09′05–dc20   90–71446

Book design by Sarabande Press
Chapter title art by Albrecht Dürer

Manufactured in the United States of America
9   8   7   6   5   4

Contents

Foreword

ALVIN TOFFLER

The fact that my friend Jacques Attali is unknown to most Americans, including most American thinkers and policy-makers, is a measure of America's intellectual provincialism. Jacques Attali was for nearly ten years the man who sat directly outside the office of French President François Mitterrand; the man who accompanied him at his meetings with Soviet President Mikhail Gorbachev and other world leaders, whispering ideas and helping to introduce Mitterrand to the twenty-first century.

Attali is now president of the European Bank for Reconstruction and Development. This is the institution created to help Eastern Europe make the painful transition from its centrally planned economies to workable market-based ones. This much at least has been reported in the American press.

What remains largely unknown, even by sophisticated

Americans, is that Jacques Attali, in what might be called his alternative life, is one of Europe's premier intellects—a man who possesses enormous energy, sparkle, drive, imagination, and ideas. Ideas, and still more ideas, plus a ravenous curiosity revealed in the subjects of the fifteen books he has written, many at four o'clock in the morning before he headed off for his desk at the Elysée Palace.

I first became aware of Attali when I heard of his book *Anti-Economics*. Wonderful, I thought. It's about time someone took on conventional economics and delivered a swift kick to its hardened categories. He was a product of France's most prestigious *grandes écoles*, precision-tooled to become a high-level bureaucrat, prepared for a lifetime devoted to scrupulous observance of the rules, yet he was willing to question some of the most fundamental assumptions of mainstream economics. Score One.

I was unaware at the time that he had also written two books on political models and the interaction of politics and economics. These were followed by a study of technology. So far, his career appeared to be more or less "respectable." But what was one to make of a trained bureaucrat who took time off to write *Bruits* (a title that could be translated as *Noise*), a work actually devoted to the politics and economics of music? And not to the economics of today's music industry. Instead, it is a deeply philosophical rumination on the relationship of music to political culture from ancient times to the present, with all sorts of strange, original insights lighting up the book's horizon.

Or what about his parallel study of the political role of medicine in society? Or his work of economic history, *Les Trois Mondes*? Or, even more surprising and interesting, his book on the history of concepts of time? Hardly what one might expect of a conventional economist or government official.

By now Mitterrand had been elected president of France, and Jacques was ensconced outside his office. So close, in fact, that to reach his own desk Mitterrand had to pass by Jacques'. The first time I visited him at the Elysée he apologized to me with a twinkle in his bespectacled eye, saying that we might have to vacate his office for a few minutes when President Mitterrand, accompanied by the then-president of Italy, needed to pass through. Together we ducked for a few seconds into what seemed like a narrow, secret corridor, as the two heads of state strolled by in private conversation. We then returned to Jacques' desk to continue our chat.

Since then, Jacques has written *A Man of Influence,* a sympathetic biography of the international banker Siegmund Warburg; a book on the nature of property; two novels about eternity; and further historical studies. Put these together and a picture emerges of a sparkling intellect impatient with the conventional wisdom of our time—a controversial figure in European intellectual life, now presiding over a $12 billion bank that could turn out to be a pillar of the new global order. Jacques is that rare figure in today's world, an intellectual idea-man who can put his ideas into action. As such, he is dealing with Europe's most critical issue—the changed relationship between Western and Eastern Europe.

It is within this context that I recommend *Millennium,* a short, pithy, significant book about, among other things, America's future in a world Attali pictures as increasingly dominated by Europe and Japan. It is a book that is by turns unsettling and exhilarating. Whether he is talking about the normalcy of crisis, or discussing the "nomadic objects" that in his opinion will be the main products of tomorrow's economy, or outlining the eight successive shifts of world economic power and the coming of what he calls the "ninth market form," or arguing that the key machines of tomorrow will be those that empower the consumer to become a producer of her or his own services, Attali is always scintillating, always crackling with creative intelligence.

There are many ideas in these pages with which I might well disagree. But there are few from which I cannot learn. Attali has things to teach us all. Especially Americans.

LOS ANGELES
March 8, 1991

I

The Coming World Order

ISTORY IS accelerating. What was beyond the grasp of imagination yesterday, except perhaps in the fertile minds of futurists and fiction writers, has already happened today. The Berlin Wall has crumbled; test-tube fertilization is routine, and a camel herder in sub-Saharan Africa can speak on a palm-sized cellular phone to a suburban commuter in Los Angeles. Future shock is yesterday. Change is the only constant in a world in upheaval. The old geopolitical order is passing from the scene and a new order is being born. That order is likely to bear little resemblance to the familiar world of the last half of the twentieth century. In the next millennium, humanity's fate will be shaped by a new set of winners and losers.

This modest essay is an attempt to sketch the contours of a

future whose broad outlines can already be glimpsed on today's horizon. It is less an argument than a series of assertions, a set of exploratory reflections. I have deliberately chosen to risk oversimplification, exaggeration, perhaps even vulgarization, in the attempt to portray the era we are about to enter. I am aware that by doing so I shall be presenting only a caricature of a deeply complex social and economic reality. But generalization has its virtues, some of them considerable, for generalization is akin to satellite photography, which reveals the outlines of vast continents and even particular buildings, while failing to indicate their contents. These musings rely on a theory of successive social orders to illuminate the extraordinary transition to the next century, which now envelops us. In this exercise, Marx's *Das Kapital* or Adam Smith's *Wealth of Nations* may be less useful than Ridley Scott's celluloid fantasy *Blade Runner*, a Hollywood confection that contains more truth about the coming age than do these classics.

In the next century, Japan and Europe may supplant the United States as the chief superpowers wrangling for global economic supremacy. Only a radical transformation of American society can forestall this development and its political consequences. From their privileged technological perches, they will preside over a world that has embraced a common ideology of consumerism but is bitterly divided between rich and poor, threatened by a warming and polluted atmosphere, girdled by a dense network of airport metropolises for travel, and wired for instant worldwide communication. Money, information, goods, and people will move around the world at dizzying speeds.

Severed from any national allegiance or family ties by microchip-based gadgets that will enable individuals to carry out for themselves many of the functions of health, education, and security, the consumer-citizens of the world's privileged regions will become "rich nomads." Able to participate in the liberal market culture of political and economic choice, they will roam the planet seeking ways to use their free time, shopping for information, sensations, and goods only they can afford, while yearning for human fellowship, and the certitudes of home and community that no longer exist because their functions have become obsolete. Like New Yorkers who every day face homeless beggars who loiter around automated teller machines pleading for spare change, these wealthy wanderers will everywhere be confronted by roving masses of "poor nomads"—boat people on a planetary scale—seeking to escape from the destitute periphery, where most of the earth's population will continue to live. These impoverished migrants will ply the planet, searching for sustenance and shelter, their desires inflamed by the ubiquitous and seductive images of consumerism they will see on satellite TV broadcasts from Paris, Los Angeles, or Tokyo. Desperately hoping to shift from what Alvin Toffler has called the slow world to the fast world, they will live the life of the living dead.

Like all past civilizations, which sought to endure by establishing an order to ward off the threat of nature and other men, the coming new order will be based on its ability to manage violence. Unlike previous orders, however, which first ruled by religion, and then by military force, the new order will manage violence largely by economic power. Of course, remnants of the once-predominant orders based on religion and military might will continue to persist, especially in the peripheral developing countries: Iran and Iraq are obvious examples.

Saddam Hussein's invasion of Kuwait and the war his act provoked serves as a useful reminder that the end of the Cold War has not settled all problems of border disputes, nationalist yearnings, and power politics. Such problems will continue to plague us far into the future. Other aggressive acts in parts of the world with less vital resources and symbolic importance than the Middle East will surely occur in the future. Military force will continue to hold sway in many areas of the impoverished world. But such events, while explosive, bloody, and dramatic, will be anachronistic affairs, sideshows only marginally relevant to the main thrust of history.

The Persian Gulf confrontation, for example, has served to distract attention from the momentous shift now taking place in the world balance of power. It has made it possible for some to insist that the United States remains the most powerful country in the world, and that predictions of its decline (and even demise) are premature, to say the least. These observers, however, are right only in the short term. For the ills that beset American society are likely to grow in severity, making it difficult for the United States to maintain its imperial posture without embracing the path of wholesale economic restructuring. Paul Kennedy, author of *The Rise and Fall of the Great Powers,* argues that the impressive projection of massive American military force halfway across the world blurs rather than illuminates the larger question of America's real position as a fading hegemonic power, not a revived one. He compares America's deployment, however justified, to Spain's decision in 1634 to send its powerful army to defend its beleaguered Hapsburg cousins during the Thirty Years' War: "Spain's infantry and generals were first-rate, its deployment via Milan, the Alps, and the upper Rhine was swift and professional. No other European nation at the time could equal such 'force projection'; Spain, it was clear, was still 'Number One.'" Yet, Kennedy notes, the Spanish monarchy was sagging under massive debts and inefficient industries, dependent upon foreign manufacturers, and beholden to special interests at home. Despite the glittering display of its armed might, by the 1640s "the suspension of interest payments and declarations of bankruptcy by the Spanish kings fully revealed the decline of Spanish power."

Kennedy does not fail to observe that, even as hundreds of thousands of U.S. troops were sent to Saudi Arabia, America's budget deficit for the year was rocketing past $300 billion—the largest in U.S. history. The lesson is clear: no nation can remain "Number One" generation after generation without a flourishing economic base upon which its political power must ultimately rest. Like Spain, the United States is not the first great power to be mired in massive debt even as it retains global responsibilities, although America's dramatic somersault from the world's largest creditor to its largest debtor in just a decade is almost certainly without precedent. Overextended debt has always been a sign of economic maladjustment, a telltale symptom of fatal imbalance before eventual demise. This has been so ever since the emergence of capitalism in the thirteenth century.

The extent of the U.S. debt crisis offers powerful evidence that we are already entering a transition in the world market order from one "core region" that is weakening to a new one. Economic power may be receding from America and is, in any case, flowing toward Europe and the Pacific. This is not a development that is to be welcomed. World growth will be jeopardized by American decline. The United States may find it possible to reverse this trend, but it is unlikely without radical reform. For it is every day more and more evident that the central organizing principle of the future, whatever happens at the margins, will be economic. This will become increasingly apparent as we approach the year 2000.

The rule of military might that characterized the Cold War is being replaced by the reign of the market. The liberal ideals of democracy and the market have defeated their chief rival— the historical challenge and alternative vision of society represented by communism. To be sure, a central conundrum remains: how to balance economic growth with social justice. Nevertheless, the political ideals and consumerist ideology of the West now impel peoples everywhere, especially in the industrialized world. After all, it was the popular allure of the democratic consumer society, not the official threat of nuclear annihilation, that critically undermined the legitimacy of the Soviet bloc regimes among their own people. The values of liberal pluralism and the promise of market prosperity have been joined in a consensus that now unites peoples all over the globe. That consensus, which has replaced the two ideologically antagonistic blocs, is capable of being satisfied only by a market that is organized around common consumer desires—whether or not such desires can be fulfilled. For the first time, the political demand for pluralism finds its economic echo.

As a result, the postwar strength of the American economy is likely to be seriously challenged. For in the emergent order taking root in this premillennial decade, the two military superpowers—the United States and the Soviet Union—are slouching toward relative, if not absolute, decline. As superpower nation-states, these winners of the postwar world may be the losers in the next century, inexorably shedding their status as great powers in the course of economic demise. Having overcome their strategic subordination to the rule of military force with the end of ideological hostilities between the United States and the Soviet Union, two new powers—a European sphere stretching from London to Moscow and a Pacific sphere based in Tokyo but extending as far as New York—will contest for supremacy. Each sphere will seek to best the other in an effort to become the center, or core, of the new world order. Which sphere succeeds will depend on who most profitably and efficiently produces the new goods that satisfy the desire for choice and autonomy in the first truly global marketplace. The location of the heart of the winning sphere will be decided by intense competition.

This new economic order will not be, as has been conventionally forecast by Daniel Bell and others, a "postindustrial" society where services replace industry. Rather, it will be a society that might be called "hyperindustrial"—a society in which services are transformed into mass-produced consumer goods. The effect will be similar to that which took place earlier in this century when washing clothes by hand was replaced by the washing machine, which in turn was made possible by the invention of the electric motor. Far more radically than the harnessing of steam and electricity in the nineteenth century, and perhaps more akin in impact to the discovery of fire by primitive tribes, the microchip and advances in biotechnology and genetic engineering are preparing the way for a revolutionary leap into a new age that will profoundly transform human culture.

Microchip-based technologies, such as the transistor and the computer, have already opened the way for the unprecedented industrialization of services—from communication to education to health care and security. Examples abound: the Sony Walkman, the laptop computer, the cellular phone, and the fax machine, all foreshadow in highly embryonic form the portable objects of the future—nomadic objects, if you will. These products will greatly weaken institutions, professions, and bureaucracies by permitting the individual an extraordinary degree of personal autonomy, mobility, information, and power. They will help fulfill the growing demand by consumers for more control over their lives by enabling them to technologically remove themselves from the institutional workplace. At the same time, people will be equipped with the means to perform a variety of tasks more simply and efficiently than ever before. The astonishing new information technologies will unleash formidable leaps in productivity, generating vigorous economic growth for decades to come. For the moment, the present recession obscures this underlying reality. And perhaps the deeper depression that may come will one day be seen as the necessary pains accompanying the birth of a new hyperindustrial order.

This new order will not put an end to history. It will not be a utopia, harmonious and placid. Indeed, conflict is more likely now that the Cold War has ended and the market has triumphed. For it is precisely because so much of the world now shares the same desire for a prosperous order based on choice that conflict will arise. In this respect, the twenty-first century may well resemble the nineteenth, when nation-states with similar imperial designs fought over the loot of raw materials and mercantile spoils, and over issues of national prestige. For inequality will cleave the new world order as surely as the Berlin Wall once divided East from West.

Even in the most privileged nations, not everyone will share equally in the vast riches of the new market order. For instance, a majority in the comparatively wealthier North, inundated by the stupefying flood of information and entertainment, will be reduced to weak and poor pawns, consigned to helplessly gaze with envy at the power and pleasure enjoyed by a minority. Ordinary people will gape with awe and resentment from their modest suburbs and homeless streets at the high rises of wealth and skyscrapers of power that will loom above their reach.

The riches of growth are not assured for those countries moving toward democracy in Eastern Europe and Asia. The political and economic freedoms so far won can vanish if the market economy does not deliver relatively quickly the consumer goods and basic necessities promised by the bold reforms that have demanded harsh sacrifices. The worst is not certain, but everything can go wrong in the midst of Europe's remarkable "velvet revolution." Should the Soviet Union collapse into civil war, millions of its citizens might well flee westward in an effort to escape their country's deepening immiseration. Such economic refugees would sorely test Europe's ability to successfully absorb such a flood.

Above all, the marginalization and misery of 3 billion men, women, and children in Africa, Latin America, and much of Asia, especially India and China, hangs heavily over the promise of sustained prosperity and freedom in the privileged North. While the green revolution has managed to contain starvation in most of Asia and famine is now only a localized, if dreadful, scourge in pockets of Latin America and Africa, the return of growth to the North will further widen the vast gulf between the haves and the have-nots.

The market and price for the primary exports of the South will continue to decline as raw materials become less important in the wealthy regions due to the growing importance of skills and information in industrial production. Moreover, many of the markets of the North will remain largely closed to exports from the poor South. Mexico, for example, has already dropped most trade barriers with the United States, but it will take years for Mexican products to make their way to the shelves of Safeway in the way that American goods can be seen in every corner bodega. It will take even longer for Brazilian products.

In restless despair, the hopeless masses of the periphery will witness the spectacle of another hemisphere's wealth. Particularly in those regions of the South that are geographically contiguous and culturally linked to the North—places such as Mexico, Central America, or North Africa—millions of people will be tempted and enraged by the constant stimulation of wants that can't be satisfied. And they will know that the prosperity that is not theirs partly comes at the cost of their well-being and at the price of their environment's degradation. With no future of their own in an age of air travel and telecommunications, the terminally impoverished will look for one in the North as economic refugees and migrants on an unprecedented scale. The movement of peoples has already begun; only the scale will grow: Turks in Berlin, Moroccans in Madrid, Indians in London, Mexicans in Los Angeles, Puerto Ricans and Haitians in New York, Vietnamese in Hong Kong.

If the North remains passive and indifferent to their plight, and especially if Eastern Europe is brought into the orbit of prosperity through the full force of Western generosity while the South is neglected, the peoples of the periphery will inevitably enter into revolt, and one day, war. They will seek to breach the equivalent of the new Berlin Wall, which the

North is even now building to seal off the South. This will be a war unlike any seen in modern times; it will resemble the barbarian raids of the seventh and eighth centuries when Europe was defeated and sank into what came to be called the Dark Ages.

But there is an even more ominous and less visible threat on the horizon. It has to do with the very warp and woof of the new world order and its liberal ideology of consumerism and pluralism. The essence of both democracy and the market is choice. Both offer the citizen-consumer the right to adopt or reject options, whether candidates or commodities, politicians or products. To reelect or to vote out of power, to hire or to fire, to change management or to shift investment—this capacity to change or reverse or alter or switch policies, people, and products—is the principal feature of the culture of choice on which the consumerist consensus rests. It informs both our political system and our economic order. Both are rooted in pluralism, and what might be called (perhaps awkwardly) the principle of reversibility. We have come to believe that nothing is (or should be) forever. Everything can be exchanged or discarded. Such a principle, however convenient in the short term, cannot anchor a civilization. Indeed, it undermines the chief imperative of all previous civilizations: to endure. Whether ruled by religious orders or royal lineages, previous civilizations have generally acted under the sign of stewardship. Native Americans, to cite but one example, often spoke of organizing their society with the "seventh unborn generation" in mind. Past leaders or rulers tended to think in terms of centuries, not in terms of quarterly earnings reports or electoral cycles.

Octavio Paz has said that "while primitive civilizations lasted for millennia, modern civilizations, which idolize change, explode within two or three centuries." Czeslaw Milosz worries that the nihilistic indifference resulting from the constant flux of change has left Western civilization running an exhausting race "between disintegration and creativity . . . hardly surviving from decade to decade."

The social vertigo induced by the principle of reversibility, which sanctifies the short term and makes a cult of immediacy, is already provoking reaction. The broad revival of religious fundamentalism, whether of the East or the West, the fanatic rejection of industrial life by radical ecologists, the nostalgia for hierarchical social structures and traditions, raise the specter that the democratic values and market principles inherent in the culture of choice will be constantly attacked, perhaps even overturned. It is not impossible to imagine any number of nightmarish scenarios—from eco-dictatorship under a charismatic green despot, to Solzhenitsyn's backward Slavic republic. The nihilistic, alienated consumer society might well trigger a revolt of considerable force and popular appeal.

To avert this possibility, the market and democracy will

have to be bound. They must be circumscribed not by conservative values that preserve the past, but by conserving values that preserve the future. For example, the culture of choice must not be allowed to embrace processes that would irreversibly alter and transform the core of life itself, through tinkering with the coding of DNA, or by continuing to destroy the rainforests, which will ultimately strip the planet of its diverse genetic heritage. These essential processes of life must be regarded as a sanctuary, a sacred preserve of the essence of life.

If we are to salvage a livable world from the new one that is emerging and avoid the growth mania that may well make civilization itself the grand loser of the next millennium, we must rethink the rules of political economy and the global balance of power. These rules must be rooted in an understanding both of the history of civilizations and of the cultural mutation of the future being wrought by radical technological innovations. We cannot permit ours to become an age that pushes, and perhaps fatally transgresses, the limits of the human condition—a condition bounded in all previous civilizations by biological borders and what Ivan Illich has called the self-limiting "earthy virtue" of place.

The great paradox of a global consumer democracy is that the right to pleasure and happiness, the right to choice in the present, may well be a toxic elixir we are forcing our children to drink. If man, the marginal parasite, turns the earth into a dead artifact, the dream of material pleasure will have murdered life itself. In order to survive the triumph of our secular ideals, we need a new definition of the sacred.

To understand the future that faces us, to make sense of the bewildering facts that surprise us with every passing day, we must build bridges between today's social sciences. For it is impossible to explain the events of today or to say something about tomorrow without a theoretical framework that allows us to untangle and interpret the history of social relations and, above all, the history of the relationship with violence that determines them all. Any such model is necessarily artificial since it risks, in the words of Fernand Braudel, "mutilating and manipulating a much more complex economic and social reality." Still, I will not hesitate to embark on a quick and necessarily sketchy tour of humanity's memory, mixing history and science. The theories that underlie this all-too-schematic romp through history are rooted in the work done by Fernand Braudel, George Dumezil, René Girard, Claude Levi-Strauss, Ilya Prigogine, Michel Serres, Yves Stourdze, and Immanuel Wallerstein.

I am convinced that the emerging world order, like those before it, is governed by laws of life and of history. Let us begin at the beginning.

Man has communicated with man for a million years. It has been at least 500,000 years since the discovery of fire. Since then people have known that they can understand and act to change their environment. It has been 15,000 years since people learned the principles, or myths, that make social life possible. It has been only 10,000 years since people began to live in villages, in a sedentary state. Finally, it has been less than 1,000 years since money has dominated a portion of humanity's social relations. How can we hope to understand what we are today without analyzing what we have learned from this distant past, and what the human brain has stored away since then in order to survive?

First, some definitions:

I will call any grouping of people that is organized to last—family, tribe, village, city, country, or international organization—a social form. In order to sustain themselves, men in all social forms have had to learn to live with violence—both the violence that comes from other men, and that which comes from nature. All early societies fight these two kinds of violence by means of myths. These myths express a basic wisdom: Violence between individuals—they seem to insist over and over—is the result of rivalry, itself provoked by confrontation over the same desirable object. The war with Troy, fought over Helen, is an example. One wants something only if another also wants it. Where there is identical desire, there is violence.

To reduce the rivalry that threatens to destroy a social form, men have organized themselves into hierarchies. They make up categories of value and distinction that allow all members of the group to visit their violence upon one person—scapegoat and prince—at the same time. By placing the right to violence in a single ruler, order is achieved among the members of the group. The order of the sacred is born from this investiture of violence and desire.

Violence caused by the invisible forces of nature is controlled in the same way as violence caused by men: the selection of an individual who, endowed by the gods with special powers, is sent to the underworld to plead the cause of the living. For this reason, in all early societies, the prince and the priest are fused together as a sort of quasi-god, who is then actually or symbolically sacrificed so that the group can survive. It is his duty to resolve disputes among men, and to intercede with the gods.

There is no orderly society without sacrifice. Nor order without disorder. But, to function permanently, this sacrifice must be described in a myth that priests repeat, and that princes obey. A notion of the sacred brings order to violence. Ever since the first sedentary social forms—perhaps 10,000 years before our time—there have been three ways to control violence: the religious, the military, and the economic. The first mediates man's relations with nature and the fact of death, the second the relationships between social forms, and the third the relationships within each social form.

These three ways of controlling violence define an order, corresponding to a certain type of social form, or social structure. These orders, which can also be called orders of the sacred, of force, and of money, succeed each other, feeding on the one that preceded it. From time to time, one or another is predominant, without excluding the others. This evolution from one order to the next does not occur in clearly delineated or separated stages. Multiple forms of the order of the sacred continue to be present in the order of force, and these two orders are themselves submerged in the order of money, which shapes the world we live in today. The functional trilogy of power remains with us today.

This is so because we have never escaped from the necessity to negotiate with violence. With the gradual extension of the size of social forms and structures, the control of violence is no longer founded on religion alone, but becomes partly political and economic, as well. The link to violence and to death oscillates between the sacred and force when great empires are built, then between force and money when capitalism emerges.

Ten thousand years ago, people lived in small, scattered groups. Myths organized the social order, which was centered on a single scapegoat. That individual was at first a real flesh-

and-blood human being, elevated above the others and endowed with special powers of intervention and authority. The chief, for example, is the priest; he restrains violence within the group by the position he assigns to each person—man, woman, child—in relation to the sacred. Everything lives: nature as well as man-made objects. There is a spirit that dwells within every object. To exchange objects is to exchange lives; in order to survive, one has to eat the flesh of animals or the bounty of plants; finding nourishment in the energy of others was, in the first order, a kind of cannibalism. In the order of the sacred, one lives by consuming lives or, what is the same thing, by the acquisition of objects. There is nothing—birth, death, art, private life—that is not integrated in this worldview.

Beginning four thousand years ago, due to agricultural and demographic necessity, villages joined together. In Babylonia, in Egypt, in China, in India, in Japan, in America, in Africa, the order of force emerged to supplement the sacred as a way of channeling rivalries and mediating competing desires. The policeman took over the role of the priest to separate and punish deviants, the marginal, the new scapegoats. The prince assumed eternal powers; he reigned at first as a god and then, in his own interest, by force. Only he could accumulate objects to use for his eternal role. Only he left evidence of his passing by a tomb: the birth of the individual occurred with the prince. Others died anonymously. Objects no longer lived; their spirits were extinguished; they became products whose trade was regulated by the police. The order of force held sway even as the order of money began to emerge in the seventh century B.C. The order of money would not finally triumph over the order of force until some twenty centuries later.

In the year A.D. 1000, in some small European ports, far from the great empires of Asia, the idea of money took hold of man's imagination. Money introduced the idea that all things could be explained by one unique measurement, one universal standard. It radically simplified the exchange and manipulation of information. Rivalry between men thus devolved upon the quantity of money that each person possessed. The use of money developed rapidly because it was a tremendous advance over all previous ways of controlling violence. The value of things was no longer the measure of the life of those who had made them, or of the force of those who owned them. Instead, money stood for things. It permitted many more objects to be traded over greater distances and allowed the creation of wealth in better conditions than ever before. Objects could circulate without threatening the life of those who traded them.

Money (otherwise known as the market, or again as capitalism—all names for inextricably linked concepts) imposed itself as a radically new way of controlling violence, superior to the older orders of the sacred and of force. In the order of money, power was measured by the amount of money one controlled—at first by force, obviously, then by the law. The scapegoat is he who is without money, and who threatens order by challenging money's distribution. It is no longer the possessed, as in the order of the sacred, nor the deviant, as in the order of force, but the beggar or poor or nomad who become the scapegoat in the order of money.

In contrast to the two preceding orders, where multiple social forms could coexist, cheek-by-jowl, as it were, in rival empires around the world, the order of money was organized at any given moment around a unique social form with a global imperative, or mission. The various social forms of the order were linked together by merchandise, which channeled the violence between them. The rule of money reigned, shaping the law of relations, in those intersecting realms between social forms.

Since about the thirteenth century, when what could be called a capitalist market order emerged, there have been a series of successive economic structures, or forms, around which society has tended to organize. Each has been based on a specific technology—usually a technology of communication, energy, or transportation. This technology, in turn, is the economic engine propelling supply and demand. Broadly speaking, there have been eight such forms since the 1300s.

Because today we are entering into a new market form— the ninth—we need to understand what defines such a form.

. . .

AT THE center of each form is a dominant city where the essential financial, technical, cultural, and ideological (but not necessarily political) power is concentrated. An elite typically controls the market—the prices and the products; the elite accumulates the profits, controls the salaries and the workers, finances artists and explorers. The elite defines the ideology that supports its power. Religious revolutions are often determining factors. The currency of the center dominates international exchanges. Artists come from everywhere to build palaces and tombs, to paint portraits and landscapes.

Around this center is a milieu, or hinterland, comprising many countries or developed regions that buy the products of the center. Here you find ancient or future centers, the regions in decline or on the rise.

Farther away is the periphery, still partially ruled by the order of force, which contains the exploited regions that sell their primary resources and their labor to the center and to the hinterland without ever having access to the wealth of the center.

Each market form uses technologies that are more efficient than its predecessors in utilizing energy and organizing communications. A form is stable so long as it creates enough wealth to maintain the demand for its products. When its ability to do this is hampered, or falters, the market form weakens. It becomes vulnerable to the challenge of an alternative form that begins to emerge, upsetting the established hierarchy of nations and of the dominant technology.

A market form thus has a relatively short life of stability, sandwiched as it is between two long-lasting periods of disorder. Disorder, it may be said, is the natural state of the world; the stability provided by an organized market form is the exception, not the rule. At any moment, market society is either in the process of separating itself from an older form, or approaching a new form. The long period of uncertainty and apparent regression between two forms is called a crisis. It begins when it becomes necessary to spend too much value to create and sustain demand—that is, to maintain consumers in a solvent state—and when too much is spent on military expenses to protect the market form. The crisis lasts until, somewhere, new technology, new ways of thinking, and new social relations generate demand more efficiently and can reduce the proportion of costs to total added value. It ends when a new form organizes, when a new center is founded, when technologies and social relations allow competing businesses on the market to replace a nonmarket service by a new mass-produced object on the market, thereby creating added value.

Thus, each crisis contains the interplay of rival countries dreaming of dominating the world or, more simply, of improving their place in the hierarchy of nations. The essential elements of international relations may be explained by the strategies employed by countries to stay in the hinterland, or to become the center, or else to escape from the periphery, or, finally, for entering the periphery when they are still outside the market order.

Today, we are at the end of one crisis and at the dawn of just such a mutation. To understand what this transition will entail, let's examine some of the characteristics of previous market forms.

FROM THE thirteenth century to the twentieth century, eight successive forms emerged, characterized by:

*eight centers: Bruges (1300); Venice (1450); Antwerp (1500); Genoa (1550); Amsterdam (1650); London (1750); Boston (1880); and New York (1930).

*eight major technological innovations, the principal ones being the printing press, accounting methods, stern steering mechanisms, the flyboat, the caravel, the steam engine, the internal combustion motor, the electric motor.

As technology is invented, production improves and society is able to cut the costs of goods and services. New mass-produced goods replace labor-intensive services previously performed outside the market, and new wealth is created. For example, the oxcart or horse-drawn wagon is replaced by the car; the washtub by the washing machine; telling stories around the fireplace by the theater; the theater by television. The relentless logic of the ever-expanding market demands that high-cost, labor-intensive services and goods be replaced by services and goods that will accomplish more with less. With each successive market form, the original unit of production and consumption—the family—is progressively reduced to its biological nucleus as its primordial functions (whether the feeding, clothing, sheltering, educating, or amusing of its young) are transferred to the market. Today the family is in danger of extinction as the services its members once provided each other for nothing are replaced by mass-produced objects that must be bought.

Braudel understood this process very well: "A world-economy always has an urban center of gravity, a city, as the logistic heart of its activity. News, merchandise, capital, credit, people, instructions, correspondence all flow into and out of the city. Its powerful merchants lay down the law, sometimes becoming extraordinarily wealthy." But Braudel knew that nothing was forever: "The besetting sin of these pulsating capitalist cities was their high cost of living, not to mention the constant inflation resulting from the intrinsic nature of the higher urban functions." Thus, he concluded, "Dominant cities did not dominate forever; they replaced each other. . . . Such shifts . . . are always significant; they interrupt the calm flow of history . . . revealing the precariousness of the previous equilibrium and the strengths of that which was replacing it. . . . There is only room for one center at a time in a world-economy. The success of one sooner or later means the eclipse of the other."

The essential question that must be answered is, Who decides which region or city will become a center?

A city becomes a center when a constellation of industrial and political elites organize themselves around a cultural project and harness their resources to develop new technologies and faster means of communication. Because of their innovative temperament and technological inventiveness, they are better suited than any other group in the world at a certain historical moment to satisfy a perceived universal need with a new product. In general, it takes a nation that is able to react in a more imaginative way than its competitors to turn a problem into a solution. For example, Amsterdam, without enough land to grow wheat, developed the dye industry in the seventeenth century. The lack of adequate coal resources in England was perhaps the chief reason for the extensive use of the steam engine.

Such events often occur at the same time as a radical change in religious thinking or in political organization: Luther and Locke are at least as important to the emergence of Amsterdam and London as the technological innovations of the time. Today, in the same way, Tokyo, unable to expand geographically, has learned to master the techniques of miniaturization. The cliché that necessity is the mother of invention is an enduring economic truth. Material abundance or geographical advantage rarely accounts for the emergence of a center.

It is important to stress that neither in past market forms nor in those that will arise in the future is the center ordained to become the master of global politics. Rather, it has often been those who have known how to avoid becoming entangled in a war that bled their rivals that have become the center. (This lesson is one we will keep in mind as we try to evaluate America's future place in the world.)

The eighth market form took shape in the 1930s. Its center was New York, the de facto capital of a region whose prosperity was being driven by the technology of the electric motor, which made possible such timesaving, mass-produced consumer durables as the washing machine, the refrigerator, and the vacuum cleaner. The Second World War was the midwife of this market form. The desire of families for homemaking durables was met by the Keynesian, New Deal social-spending policies of the early postwar period that, above all, sought to put purchasing power and home ownership into the hands of the majority of Americans. Easy credit meant consumers could always buy new products. Madison Avenue and Wall Street did their best to create and expand the markets for products of all kinds. The market form whose center was New York achieved a remarkable hegemony until the mid-1960s, when it entered a crisis as the cost of producing goods and services increased drastically. Disorder erupted in the markets of the principal currencies of the center and of its surrounding hinterland. This crisis will last until a new center and new consumer goods emerge.

The model of how world centers develop and decline helps us to understand the period of transition we are now entering. It offers particular insight into the efforts of the United States to stem its removal as the country that contains the center of the eighth market form and prevent the rise of its challengers in Europe and Japan who seek to establish themselves as the location of the new center of a triumphant ninth market form.

The Struggle for Supremacy

ICTATORSHIPS are collapsing throughout the world, on every continent and in every hemisphere. No tyrant is able any longer to seal himself off successfully from the tide of democracy. Electronic communications and television render borders porous. Traditional notions of national sovereignty are increasingly irrelevant. The fax machine and the videocassette make it possible to pierce the veil of state censorship. Nevertheless, even if the world seems daily to be growing closer, more homogeneous in its cultural values and material aspirations, even if large corporations are establishing themselves in all countries, power remains in the hands of an elite. An elite, moreover, that resides in those few places where power and wealth accumulate, where the critical questions facing the planet are decided.

The eighth market form, whose center is New York, is rent by a severe crisis. It faces fierce competition. Other regions of the world desire to become the center of a new market form. It is, of course, too early to predict with certainty where the future center of the world-economy will be. But we can see already a new world struggling to be born, heralding a new age of development. The culture of choice, or to put it in other words, the imperative of the market and democracy, is itself acting as midwife to the emerging ninth market form. The ability to create, to produce, to trade is inextricably bound up with the spread of political pluralism. What is going on in the streets and parliaments of Budapest and Soweto, in Santiago and Moscow, reflects this evolutionary process.

This evolution will disturb present-day economic and national-security arrangements, and will alter the rules of geostrategy, for in the aftermath of the ideological hostility of the Cold War, geography will again impose its laws on history. For the past half century, the world order has been organized around what might be described as a pyramid and two pillars. The pyramid is the shape taken by the eighth market form of the order of money. At its summit is the United States, with all other nations arranged in descending and hierarchical fashion around the American peak. The dollar ruled international currency, American popular culture reigned supreme. This basic fact has been the starting point for all thought and theory about the modern political economy.

The two pillars, vestiges of the order of force, have been the two principal nuclear powers—the United States and the Soviet Union—who imposed their views on their respective alliances and were arbiters of regional conflicts. This basic fact has been the starting point for all thought and theory about contemporary military strategy.

Today, this structure is dissolving before our eyes: the pyramid is changing its summit; one of the pillars is crumbling. America's position as the peak is under severe strain; in Eastern Europe, the order of force is giving way to the order of money. These developments are profoundly changing the nature of global economic struggle and military conflict. Soon one will no longer be able to speak strictly of North-South, or East-West. The old Cold War categories no longer pertain.

It would be foolhardy to believe that either the utter demise of the United States or the complete dissolution of the Soviet Union are irreversibly established. It is only certain that the new center, in the sense given to this word in the preceding chapter, will consolidate somewhere in the two dominant spheres—Europe or the Pacific rim—and that Eastern Europe will rejoin the market economy. For the rest, everything depends on the way that changes are managed. The United States may host the center once again, but this would require a herculean effort of national will in order to effectively harness the country's assets. That effort, in the degree that is required, will be difficult. If America's economic decline hardens into reality, Europe will suffer. But, if Western Europe is able to link Eastern Europe with its development, an integrated Europe has a chance to assume the role of the center of the world economy. It will then be able to develop as the most populated, the richest, and the most creative center in the world.

If not, the new center will likely be Japan, for that island nation combines the necessary conditions for attracting global monetary, industrial, and even cultural power. Japan has several advantages over America and Europe: the mass production of high-technology consumer products has been developed there longer than anywhere else; there is a coherent compact of state and industry with a common will to take, maintain, and expand market share; there is an indigenous cultural tradition of self-mastery, an obsession to create consensus among its people; and, finally, there is enormous influence over a hinterland (read: the United States of America and the Asian Tigers—Hong Kong, Singapore, South Korea, and Taiwan), which is already advanced.

These two emerging contenders for the role of center of the ninth market form have embarked on a vigorous competition. The stakes are high, for they are nothing less than the economic and political mastery of the world. Neither has yet triumphed over the other. Inside each of these competing spheres, one can see a considerable growth in trade and merchandise, in people, in information; this interior growth is even more rapid than that of external trade. Each sphere forms a homogenous, closed group. In each, the principal economic power—Japan on one side, the European Community on the other—is moving ahead of the principal military power: the United States on one side, the Soviet Union on the other. A process of increased integration and intensified rivalry is shaping this evolution.

To understand where this double movement might lead, and which of these two spheres will ultimately dominate the other, it is useful to clarify certain facts and trends present in each of them. By Pacific sphere, I mean the group formed by the Pacific rim countries, that is to say (in a general sense), Oceania: the rapidly developing countries of East Asia (Japan, South Korea, Malaysia, Indonesia, Singapore, Taiwan, the Philippines, Hong Kong) and all the nations of North and South America. I do not include China or Vietnam. This enormous region has become a place of economic explosion. Populations and production are growing rapidly, transportation grids are multiplying, and internal commerce is growing more rapidly than trade with the rest of the world. We are witnessing the formation of a truly integrated economic sphere; power is shifting from one coast of the Pacific to the other.

However, there are important conditions that any candidate for the center of the next world-economy must fulfill, conditions that Japan especially may find difficult to meet. For example, can Japan create social values that peoples the world over can embrace? Is Japan willing to assume the role of military protector of the periphery and of the hinterland, a role the center must fulfill? The answers are not at all obvious, especially after Japan's passive behavior during the Gulf War. For the first time in the history of capitalism, a nation that could become the center hesitates to pay the price and bear the burden of assuming an imperial mantle. The lesson of history, which teaches that the summit is the point that is closest to the precipice, has been particularly well learned in Japan.

Certainly the United States does not intend to retire voluntarily from center stage. And, to be sure, America is blessed with considerable financial, technological, and demographic resources. Nevertheless, unless dramatic changes occur, it just doesn't have sufficient means to win decisively against Japan.

The predominant phenomenon in the United States today is the nation's continuing relative economic decline. Many people still refuse to believe it. Pundits have taken to citing Washington's victory over Baghdad as proof positive that the devotees of decline couldn't be more wrong. They look at the power of the United States in nuclear warheads, its vast military equipped with every conceivable technological advantage. They estimate the power of its aerospace industry, observe the power of the dollar, evaluate its market share, dream about the still-substantial wealth of Wall Street, consider the size of its banks (however shaky their foundations may be), envy the clout of its capitalist economy, admire the creativity of Hollywood, and much more besides. When they are told that America is in decline, they answer that the decreasing role of the United States in the world economy is due to the rebuilding of the countries that were devastated by the Second World War and not due to any fundamental weakness of America. The land of the brave and the home of the free, they insist, remains as powerful and as dynamic as ever. Finally, they argue, even if America's economy should slip into severe decline, the country will know how to spur itself forward enough to regain the initiative, to recapture its leading role. Besides, America is Europe's daughter, it is said, and therefore is permanently turned toward the Atlantic and the Mediterranean, not toward the Pacific.

None of these arguments are convincing, unfortunately. Industry is the only lasting foundation of a country's power, and it is in this sense that the signs of America's relative decline are seen everywhere. This is regrettable, for it is better for Europe and the world that America remain healthy and strong. But facts are facts.

For example, American industrial productivity (still the strongest in the world) has grown at a rate that is three times slower than that of Japan's, and two times slower than Europe's. Not one new product that has appeared in the past few years was made in the United States, with the notable exception of the microprocessor. Even traditional consumer goods are no longer manufactured in any competitive way. The United States exports almost no automobiles or televisions or household appliances made in the United States. For products that use modern technology, which comprise perhaps two thirds of U.S. exports and three quarters of American production, the commercial balance is increasingly in deficit. For high-technology products, the United States has only a positive trade balance in those two sectors in which it has had a semimonopoly for a long time, but not for much longer: aerospace and computers. For all other products, the deficit has increased sixfold in ten years. Even in the arms industry, in aerospace and in computers, where the United States is at the cutting edge, competing enterprises multiply in other countries, presaging a drop in America's share of those few markets that it still dominates. Of course, American companies have overseas branches that are not included in commercial statistics, unless under the heading of repatriated profits to the home office. But, what is not made in the United States proper only provides indirect benefits to the American economy.

The economic deficit has grown, while America's role in the global economy has shrunk: in the past fifteen years,

American industry lost six percentage points of its share of the world market. Japan, in the same period, gained fifteen points. America's share of the market for machine tools—an essential product indicative of a country's economic competitiveness—has fallen from 25 percent to 5 percent in thirty years, while that of Japan has increased from 0 percent to 22 percent.

To finance this deficit, the United States has supported the growing use of the dollar by foreign lenders, and in a floating currency value system the dollar has become the universal measure of value, both for payment and for reserves. Because of this, the external debt of the United States has increased massively, now surpassing its lending abroad. The enormous rise in the cost of its educational, health, and defense budget makes it impossible to support without deficit financing. Bridges, roads, schools, and hospitals deteriorate and cry out for repair. To avoid increasing taxes, the American society has reduced its investment in infrastructure (which has reduced the efficiency of the market economy) and has borrowed on the market—which is to say, mostly from Japan—the amounts necessary to finance its deficit. American savings are declining more and more, making it difficult to finance investment in the future. Private financial sources seem unable to react to this development. They channel loans to traditional industries rather than toward innovative enterprises, toward foreign borrowers rather than toward domestic borrowers, toward big business rather than toward small concerns, toward agriculture rather than toward industry.

Increasing cost of services, decreasing savings, a growing number of beggars, criminals, and drug addicts, loss of enthusiasm for industry, a weak long-term vision of the world market for consumer goods: America is not doing enough to produce the goods it will need, nor to export what is required to finance and reduce its debt. These distressing developments are rooted in a profound cultural mutation—the cult of immediate gratification, the lack of internationalism, the weakness of global social solidarity, all reflect a country abandoning those values for which it is so universally admired.

This predicament may be changed by a relaunching of an effort to invest in industry and in the infrastructure needed for an efficient market economy, a rise in savings, the arrival of new products, or a conquering commercial will. The use of America's southern backyard in Central and Latin America is the country's main asset. For such rejuvenation to work, however, the United States must become a Spanish-speaking nation. All this is unlikely.

The economic center of the United States will continue to move toward the South, and toward the Pacific Coast. This is due to an aspect that is completely new in the evolution under way in the United States. Its trade and commercial exchanges with Europe are not increasing at the same rate as its transpacific trade. Already the trade in the Pacific is more than half

THE STRUGGLE FOR SUPREMACY

the transatlantic trade. If it continues at the present rate, it will have doubled before the end of the century. This transpacific trade is a particularly cruel index of the relative economic decline of the United States. This is because the movement of goods is essentially one way: the American deficit with Asia comprises nearly two thirds of the total deficit of the United States and equals a third of its entire trade, some $100 billion, of which half is Japan's alone.

Many observers maintain that the U.S. deficit is explained by Japanese protectionism and by the archaic nature of Japanese distribution networks. This explanation, although partly true, seems insufficient. Of course, Japanese protection aggravates the American deficit, but it is not enough to create it: over time, protectionism cannot resist competitive products.

Thus, everything seems to indicate that in the emerging Pacific sphere, the mastery of massive investments in fundamental industries—that is economic power in its most essential aspect—today resides in Japan. In just twenty years, a nation defeated in the Second World War has passed from the level of an underdeveloped country to one of the world's great economic powers. The main evidence for this conclusion is industrial. Japanese businesses spend twice as much for modernization than their American counterparts. Japan produces more than half of the world's production of microprocessors, compared with 38 percent by the United States, the inventors of this essential element of today's technology, and 10 percent for Europe, of a world market of $500 billion. Japanese firms define the consumer goods they are going to produce and deduce from that the necessary technical progress. Since they are the creators of the major new consumer gadgets, they are able to embark on investments that do not see profits at the outset. They can also lower their prices with the single goal of expanding or maintaining their market share. Japan has known how to first imitate and then invent those objects, technologies, and styles needed by the industrial world of tomorrow. The use of robots and the miniaturization of machines were imagined elsewhere, but it was the Japanese who developed them, just as in an earlier age the steam engine was developed in England without having been invented there.

The reason for this rise in power is principally cultural: each time that a center is born, it is a cultural reaction to a geographic challenge or because of the lack of an essential resource. In Japan, for example, the paucity of habitable land favored miniaturizing objects; fear of isolation spurred the development of means of communication; lack of energy drove the research for ways to substitute information for travel; frequent earthquakes led to the invention of light, portable, inexpensive objects that could be replaced easily. Finally, because of its long history of internecine violence, Japanese society learned to manage change through consensus. The word for "change" in Japanese—*nemawashi*—

also means "transplanting." While change may be slow in coming, when it does come it takes root deeply.

These cultural and geographical conditions push the Japanese, more than any other people, to bet on the future. They are a people who save more than they spend, and export more than they import. They have a long-term vision of their interests, a capacity to work hard, the commitment to quality, an aptitude for conceiving and producing new objects of mass consumption, a desire to learn from others, and a dynamism toward the outside world.

Without any overt declaration, Japan has become the dominant pole of the Pacific sphere, a sphere that increasingly embraces the United States. Little by little, Japan has taken control of the surrounding markets and industrial and communications networks. Tokyo's industrial investments in the Asian Pacific rim have grown by a third each year; Japan now controls more than a third of the commercial networks and almost half of the distribution of today's consumer goods. In these rapidly growing countries, Japanese industries find large markets that accelerate their own growth. Few of these countries grow less than 10 percent a year. The four "dragons" of Hong Kong, Singapore, Taiwan, and South Korea have lifted themselves almost to the level of the most developed European countries. Beyond this, their population growth— and the corresponding growth in the number of consumers— is particularly rapid. Taken together, the Asian nations of the

Pacific rim already produce one sixth of the world's gross product. By the turn of the century, their gross product will equal that of the European Community or of the United States. Trade among themselves already constitutes one tenth of world trade, and considerably more of transpacific commerce. The growth of this trade is so rapid that, in ten years, half of world trade will occur in the Pacific rim. Already, six of the world's largest ports are located on the Asian side of the Pacific, and more than half of all the air transport cargo of the planet will traverse the Pacific (this traffic is expected to increase by a factor of six by the year 2000).

This trade stimulates Japan's growth enormously and deepens Japan's leading role in the economy of the sphere it dominates. Its efficiency will greatly increase by the reduction of the main handicap that retards or restrains growth in this sphere. That handicap is distance. As ever, geographic proximity to trading partners is the key for instilling an awareness of belonging to the same world and for allowing commercial habits and industrial synergies to emerge. Since the distances between Pacific neighbors is still too great to allow the exchange of ideas, of work, of goods in the same rapid and efficient way as in Europe and the United States, Japan must work hard to overcome this obstacle. A leap in the acceleration of communications is still necessary.

A communications revolution has already taken place in the transfer of information: the telephone, the fax, cables, and satellites, all allow the transmission—at any moment, to any location in the world, at virtually the speed of light—of drawings, designs, and images vital for industrial production and for individual use. It is no accident that the Japanese are leaders in this area.

Transporting goods and people across the vast expanse of the Pacific Ocean requires a new generation of planes and ships. Hypersonic airplanes that can reach speeds of Mach 3.5 and Mach 5 are being studied. If successfully commercialized, these planes will be able to reach any point in the Pacific in less than two hours from Tokyo. Several countries are competing for the privilege of being first to design and manufacture such planes, including France, Britain, Germany, the United States, and, of course, Japan. The success of these projects depends upon major technical advances in materials, propulsion, aerodynamics, structures, and fuels, as well as the design of an engine for takeoff, for transition to supersonic speeds and acceleration, reentry to the atmosphere, and landing. Whether such planes will actually be created is an open question, for they are not vital for any country beyond those of the Pacific rim. The Japanese, who are the most affected, are very actively pursuing such a development, and it is possible that they will produce the first such plane, almost certainly in cooperation with the United States. (Boeing already collaborates with Mitsubishi to manufacture the 767 and to modify the 777.) Such a plane will permit the Pacific nations to live in

MILLENNIUM

a space-time that is similar to today's unification of Europe.
Japan is preparing for such an eventuality: it plans to build
near Tokyo an artificial island where a new airport, like
Singapore's "airtropolis," will concentrate the means of communication of the future, and will be able to handle the new
hypersonic aircraft.

Similar progress is necessary and predictable in ocean ship-
ping. Fifteen years from now, ships that are much faster and
more energy efficient than those available today will make all
Asian ports less than one day apart, and will reduce the
transpacific voyage to three days. Once again, considerable
progress is required to master the necessary technology in
dynamics, materials, and propulsion. In the same way that the
galley and the flyboat helped to make Venice and Amsterdam
into world centers, Japan, if it is serious about becoming the
center of the Pacific sphere, must revive naval shipyards that
are now left to the profitable domination of South Korea.

Finally, Japan is interested in progress in ground transportation. The Japanese automobile industry already has taken a
sizable lead in the entire Pacific rim. It is expected to double
its market share in production in the United States over the
next several years. Japan is also working on revolutionary
hydrogen engines. In the next fifteen years, high-speed magnetic trains will bring all of the island's cities to within one
hour of Tokyo, thus transforming the Japanese archipelago

into one unified metropolis, a gigantic center capable of coordinating the sphere it has the ambition to control.

While it is true that geographic and cultural differences among the various countries that make up the Pacific sphere will hamper its overall integration, Japan does not find this difficulty insurmountable. With delicacy and diplomacy, Japan is slowly revealing its crushing technological, financial, and economic superiority. Mastery of the sea is clearly essential. Once Japan achieves that, it will then be able to dominate its partners. Still remaining, of course, is the problem of how this sphere will be militarily protected.

Tokyo is already a major center of global finance: it is where much of the world's profits and financial instruments are concentrated. At least eight of the world's ten largest banks are there. The system of Japanese decision making—that curious and enigmatic coalition of businessmen and high-ranking bureaucrats—demands a high level of property ownership and funds so as to control a considerable buying capability, targeted mainly at American and European businesses. The rise in the value of the yen has not slowed the invasion of world markets by Japanese products. This has helped the value of the Japanese stock market grow from 10 percent to 55 percent of the total value of the world exchanges. In the same period, the value of the U.S. exchanges dropped from 40 percent to 20 percent of the world total.

The Japanese juggernaut continues to gain strength. Because of its exports, and its export of capital, Japan accumulates each year a surplus of $200 billion, which it invests in businesses worldwide, but primarily in the United States (two thirds of Japanese bond purchases are in the United States). Japan has already bought the essential core of commercial office space, as well as many medium-sized businesses. Japanese interests already own over a third of the real estate in downtown Los Angeles, as well as a large share of that icon of American industrial preeminence, New York's Rockefeller Center. Sony and Matsushita have stunningly taken over the Hollywood dream factory through their respective purchases of Columbia Pictures and MCA. The Mitsui group, for example, owns a third of the stock of seventy-five American businesses, for a total annual revenue of $17 billion, and hopes to double the number of subsidiaries in just a few more years. In 1989, Japanese companies invested two times more than the year before in American high-technology companies or in strategic investments.

In addition, it seems increasingly clear that Japan will sooner rather than later shape (and perhaps control) the majority of images that will traverse the Pacific. Japan is likely to seize control of defining the standard for such products as high-definition television throughout the Pacific sphere, and perhaps elsewhere in the world as well. This will almost certainly occur if Europe and America do not succeed in forming a joint counterattack. Japan will then impose its products upon American consumers, selling all the television sets, all the scanners, and all the computer-aided graphic design systems. For the United States this turn of events will be critical. It will occur at the very moment that the making of images and the means of their transmission is imposing its character more and more on objects and goods and products of all kinds. If the United States proves unable to compete in this arena, it will have hastened its relative economic decline considerably.

The United States risks finding itself transformed into a kind of hinterland for a new center located in Tokyo. America may become Japan's granary, like Poland was for Flanders in the seventeenth century. More land in America is devoted to agricultural production destined for Japanese mouths than the entire land surface of Japan. Japanese savings already help pay the salaries of Washington's civil servants through financing the deficit. American universities are largely forming the scientific cadre of its principal economic rival.

The United States is unlikely to accept, in the long run, the humiliations that this subordination implies. When Americans realize what the geostrategic and cultural consequences of these developments are, they will reassess their own identity, and react with more or less good grace. Others will propose, as some already are, to batten down the hatches, to close the American economy to world (read: Japanese) competition. The day is not far away when the United States will oppose, on the basis of national security, the control of America's principal businesses by Japanese interests. Major strategic issues will then certainly arise. Japan already supplies more than a third of the key technologies for America's arsenal.

The United States can (with great difficulty) resist Japan's advance by taking an alternative route, breaking established relationships, destroying business alliances, creating a new hemispheric economic zone.

The trade with the European sphere across the Atlantic can help reverse this trend. The United States may attempt to become a part of the European sphere. And this attempt will be welcomed because it is in Europe's interest to see that America no longer declines. This will strengthen Europe in its competition with Japan.

For the immediate future, the institutional organization of the Pacific rim cannot but remain informal and ambiguous as a way of saving face over the reality of a momentous power shift. In time, the United States will surely adjust to a new identity. Perhaps by the early years of the new century, the reality can be codified in a new set of institutions. Such institutions will be required to link the diverse countries that make up the Pacific sphere. Ultimately, that sphere will become organized, but in a much different way than the European Community. The Pacific countries are hobbled by their lack of any common history. Nor do they share an intimate understanding of the models and levels of development of their neighbors. Moreover, their growing integration, despite these obstacles, will inexorably raise questions about the nature of power relationships between the United States and Japan. At the moment, and for a long time to come, neither nation is ready to address the shift in relations that answering such questions would imply. It will be in everyone's interest to try to find ways to save the face of a declining but still great power.

It is possible that Japan will decline to pursue the political role of the economic center, choosing instead to limit its influence to the western nations of the Pacific. But such a decision is redolent of its disastrous dream earlier in the century of establishing a "greater co-prosperity sphere." The peoples of the region still stagger under the weight of that memory. Still, Japan is unlikely to be able to restrain its desire for power, and ultimately it will seek to create the conditions throughout the Pacific sphere that will permit it to emerge as the center. Perhaps its current reluctance to trumpet such an ambition is disingenuous, a deliberate strategy to confuse its competitors. Perhaps it only pretends to play with the idea that it does not wish to be the center—and tells us this so that we will mistake its insistence for its intention—just so that Tokyo has a better chance to triumph over all rivals.

． ． ．

THE EVOLUTION of the European sphere is more difficult to predict. Until quite recently, its future seemed to be clear. Nineteen ninety-two was going to bring about a "fortress Europe." But the predictability of the western half of Europe moving alone toward economic integration was derailed by the unforeseen events of 1989. One Europe is possible again, but so are nationalist and irredentist splintering, conflict, and regression. Political integration in the West remains fragile, democratization in the East remains at risk, and the two parts of Europe are finding it exceedingly hard to join together economically.

Still, from the West, one can see a bloc being born at the same moment that in the East a bloc is disintegrating. Countries bouncing from the periphery to the hinterland, and simultaneously from dictatorship to democracy, hesitate to join a new bloc. But they will nevertheless be forced to do it. One day, all of Europe will be united, one way or another, replete with continental institutions. Thus, a formidable power will be born: the European sphere. Military alliances in Europe will evolve into networks of political coordination among all European countries. The primary means of transportation will be by land. Railroad technologies will be crucial. It isn't certain at this juncture who will dominate this immense region and where the center of the European sphere will be. Europe's equivalent to Japan's archipelago, wired and covered by a latticework of speed train tracks, is the region that extends from London to Milan, passing Brussels, Paris, and Frankfurt. This area seems the best placed as the candidate for the center of the European sphere. Controlling the capital cities allows this corridor, with some resistance, to determine the movement of trade and commerce.

Because it has spent decades in forced exile from the rest of Western Europe, it will be decades more before Berlin can contend for the center with the advantages of the London-Milan corridor.

The probable European center also has its handicaps. It does not control all the technologies of the future, and its population is aging. The demographic growth, creativity, and the export orientation of southern Europe pose a challenge to the dominance of this more northerly zone.

In the end, the center of the European sphere will be located in the place that develops the most advanced trans-European transportation and communication systems (by 2010, Paris and Moscow may be linked by high-speed train), becomes the center of research and innovation, and possesses the social cohesion that will best enable the management of a continent in the midst of social upheaval.

THE ISSUE of competition between the European sphere and the Pacific sphere is not yet played out. If Europe as a whole knows how to organize itself, it has tremendous assets, even if the Pacific holds a considerable lead today. Between these two spheres, rivalry will provoke commercial, financial, and political tensions, aimed at the domination of technology, businesses, and markets, in particular in their respective peripheries (Africa for Europe; Latin America and Southeast Asia for Japan).

A great deal needs to happen if Europe is really to contend seriously with Japan for the right to rule as the center of the ninth market form. If Western Europe progresses toward political unity and Eastern Europe succeeds in democratization, if the two parts of Europe can invent audacious ways of joining together, of aiding each other, then it is not impossible to imagine a European triumph over its Asian rival. With a tremendous amount of effort, creativity, and work, the ecu could surpass the dollar and the yen, the living standard in Europe could overtake the most elaborate Asian standard, and the values of European civil society—liberty and democracy—could stretch across the entire planet.

This vision may seem excessive: it already is proving difficult to absorb the countries of eastern and central Europe into the market order of the West. Nevertheless, much is being accomplished. The twelve nations involved in the construction of the European Community will build a single market, and they will draw conclusions from this process for cooperation in fiscal matters, education, scientific research, international law, business regulation, social policies, and environmental protection.

This process harbors a relentless inner logic, a logic that pushes the Western European states toward ever greater political and military integration. Already they have decided to undertake the creation of a common currency and, later on, a central bank, as well as defending the environment with transnational institutions. Later, they will consider converging their foreign policies and defense strategies. This process is irreversible unless what happens in the East, and especially in the Soviet Union, puts it all into question again. If successful, this process will permit Europe to become a political world leader, beyond its economic role.

The construction of a European sphere is made possible, of course, by the collapse of the old order of force in Eastern Europe. That collapse was unexpected only because it was so swift. It was apparent well before 1989 that there could be no wealth without creativity, and no creativity without democracy. For the Soviet Union, and therefore for Eastern Europe's Communist regimes, the choice was between dying or changing the order. The spectacle of abundance in the West, which glasnost helped to spotlight, hastened the momentum of collapse.

The challenge now is to bring the eastern parts of Europe closer to the West. For this to happen, Eastern Europe must evolve successively—for which there is cause to doubt—in three directions.

First, a civil society, with the rule of law and the constitution of democratic institutions, must be put in place. As is already happening with some speed, the Communist parties must be replaced by parties that accept pluralism and the transfer of power, subject to elections. So far, with the exception of Romania, Eastern Europe has witnessed the first nonbloody revolution in history. One worries that it cannot remain so. This is especially so in the Soviet Union. Nevertheless, whatever the outcome, however spectacular and tragic, the deeper underlying momentum pushing society toward the order of the market and democracy will persist.

Second, these countries will have to develop market economies. The transition from societies in which scarcity is managed by waiting in lines to one in which it is managed by high prices cannot occur without the dislocation of what we might call "market shock." Unemployment, inflation, and indebtedness threaten these economies emerging out of stagnation. Yet they have little choice but to confront the reality of their low level of development by handing the distributive function over to prices and putting in place a judicial framework that guarantees the autonomy of enterprises, infrastructure, and a social safety net.

This change requires a sea change in consciousness. Society, after all, is being asked to change from one in which violence is managed by force to one in which violence is managed by money. This will occur by solving problems that are similar—to use a simple example—to those of Latin

America: poorly developed distribution networks, a black market, inflation, unemployment, debt. None of these problems have instant solutions. The peoples of Eastern Europe must come to terms with the reality of their level of development and permit prices to perform their distributive function, and to put a legal system in place that will give businesses genuine decision-making power. The fact that Europe is a continent of some 700 million people is an asset for a successful transition.

Doing so will bring the risk of crises, retreats, even defeats, as we have seen, in a completely different context, in the Chinese example. Even if these reforms are carried out with courage, with a spirit of justice, and with political skill, it will take a long time for them to produce the desired results, if they ever do. Entrepreneurs will not appear overnight to create jobs, nor will capital immediately return to countries from which it was once forcibly expelled.

Political reform will endure only if accompanied by economic reforms that create decentralized and competitive centers of power in society. Otherwise, the power of decision, in a vacuum, will tend to reconcentrate, especially in reaction to the chaotic social conditions that will accompany market shock.

Third, along with the political reform that dismantles totalitarian structures, a political culture of tolerance must evolve. Lifting the lid off bureaucratic oppression has revived the hatreds and the tragedies that are so often history's most enduring legacy, from Poland to Armenia, and which scar national cultures. With the retreat of the tanks, the past has reemerged and everything must be renegotiated. Otherwise, the tanks will surely return. The reunion of people and their histories will create national, religious, linguistic, and cultural identities, including dangerously nostalgic ones, which won't necessarily respect today's map. The dreams of new alliances and new associations, reminiscent of the Austro-Hungarian Empire, of the Hanseatic League, of the Baltic states, the Prussian Empire, or the Ottoman Empire, have been incited.

The task of integrating Eastern Europe with the rest of the continent isn't assured. In a way, the Oder-Neisse line resembles a border between North and South more than East and West. The association of the East with Western Europe will only succeed if the West aids in lessening the imbalances so that convergence can work. For example, Western exports must be allowed in so that the Czechs, Poles, or Hungarians can earn foreign exchange to finance their imports. Debts must be rescheduled and interest rates reduced so that scarce capital can be used for development. Projects such as a unified telecommunications system and joint financing of a continent-wide infrastructure, a common environmental protection agency, or joint business ventures, as well as common administrative law and tax regulations, would help cement continental unity. Institutions must be created in which Eastern European countries will be equal partners of their Western counterparts.

THE FIRST pan-European institution—the European Bank for Reconstruction and Development—is already established and is capitalized at some $12 billion. In this bank, all countries on the European continent (together with Japan and America), acting as equal partners, study and finance a variety of projects. It is intended to be an apprentice shop for the transition from a centralized economy to a market economy. It will finance the great transportation and communication systems that will reduce the distance between people, ideas, and products on a continent too long divided against itself. The rapprochement between the two halves of Europe will depend on the success of these networks. The process of embarking on such continent-wide projects will itself cause a continual economic and cultural homogenization of what will one day be a European sphere. For the creation of a European confederation, for the entry of all European countries into the existing European Community, for the construction of a European "common home," the bank will play a similar role to the European Coal and Steel Community of the 1950s as the cornerstone of today's European Community.

If this process is successful, the European sphere will unify in a natural way. All the countries in the region will belong to continental institutions. Europe will have started down the path toward embracing its own common identity, escaping from ancient quarrels. The stability of this emergent European sphere depends greatly on how well a united Germany performs. For it is clear that Germany provides the link between the two parts of the continent.

IN THE twenty-first century a fierce struggle for supremacy will take place among cities, nations . . . even continents. If the ninth market form resembles the preceding eight, there will be a center surrounded by a hinterland and a periphery. The most immediate result is likely to be the continued juxtaposition of two contending spheres (the Pacific and the European) with two centers, each organized around a pair composed of a political giant and an economic giant, competing at the same time for the interior of each sphere and for the domination of the other sphere.

This evolution will bring great upheavals. Inside each sphere, the competition between the political power and the economic power will bring serious conflicts. It will be difficult for one to accept the ambitions of the other. At the same time, both will recognize how necessary close links are for each other. Therefore, a separation of power must be decided inside each sphere. In the Pacific and in Europe, questions must be asked: Who will have the dominant currency? Who will control defense? Where will the principal financial market be located? One can imagine the stronger economic power

(Japan) leaving for a time some international political responsibilities to the stronger military power (the United States). Today, these responsibilities do not have much importance with respect to the longer-term strength for those who do not have the financial wherewithal to maintain them. In reality, the current superpowers will lose control of their respective empires, and will gradually become the secondary power in their former realms.

The United States will try to halt its relative economic decline by cutting military spending in order to reduce its budget deficit. The United States will gradually continue to reduce its troop strength on its allies' territory. This reduction in arms, even if it is partial, will provide the resources for a tremendous economic rebound. We can expect a massive reduction in fixed armaments. Short-range nuclear weapons have no more reason to exist, except for secret regional ambitions. Negotiations on conventional arms reduction will accelerate, and will result in a massive removal of foreign troops still stationed on European soil.

Sadly, none of this will cause tension to disappear. Because of the lack of superpower control, territorial disputes, economic quarrels, perhaps military battles will be possible, even likely, between some of the countries in each of the two spheres. We must remember that in this century, the Europe composed of separate nations has twice been the cause and main theater of action of a world war. The frontiers that

resulted from the Second World War do not always corre-
spond with cultural or linguistic realities. No one should
forget that one day the Japanese may want to ask the Americans questions about Hiroshima. Of course, until now, no
democracy has ever gone to war against another democracy,
and this fact alone may provide the principal hope for the
future. But here is the main risk: some nations might decide
to stop being democracies in order to wage war.

It may be that neither the Pacific nor the European sphere
will triumph over the other, and that the center of the coming
world order will be divided among many regions, according
to the functions they provide: America for culture, currency,
and defense; Japan for finance and industry; Europe for life-
style and services. Such an outcome is imaginable. It could
happen for some time as the world hesitates between two rival
spheres. But such a division would not endure. History establishes a clear pattern: there can be no defense without finance,
nor currency without industry, nor life-style without culture.
We can anticipate, then, that eventually one metropolis will
incorporate all the necessary characteristics of the new market
form, whose outlines can now be glimpsed, and will, for the
first time, extend its dominion across entire continents.

THIS STRUGGLE for supremacy of the coming world order
pales in the light of potential conflicts between the two
emerging spheres and an exploited periphery, whose inhabi-

tants will be denied an opportunity to participate in the wealth of the North. This is when the struggle begins for the immense lands of Asia. India and China will refuse to fall under the sway of either the Pacific or European sphere. The Middle East is also, as we have seen, a dangerous wild card. In all these areas, the proliferation of military technology, the diversity of arms, the manufacture of chemical and biological weapons, and the ballistic missiles capable of carrying either conventional or chemical warheads make the outbreak of brief but bloody wars possible, perhaps even probable. The disappearance of competing ideologies and the generalization of the market economy stimulates similarity of desires. Violent rivalry for territories and resources may well be the paradoxical result. Lebanons may multiply. War will occur if there is no one strong enough to prevent it. Without regional institutions to act as an architecture for peace, we face a future in which spheres of abundance collide in a sea of instability.

III

Millennial Losers

HE BIG losers of the next millennium will be the inhabitants of the periphery and the biosphere itself. Outside the emerging Pacific and European spheres, 4 billion people will take faltering steps toward a market society and democracy. But the market alone cannot develop industry or build the basic infrastructure of health and education systems. The market alone cannot make raw materials profitable. Nor can it protect the environment. Nor can it close the immense and growing gap between the privileged regions and the paralyzed periphery. If the market alone is relied upon to build whole societies, it will end up producing the principal revolutionaries of tomorrow who will rise in resentment against the wealthy inhabitants of the privileged centers of the world.

Each of the emerging spheres has a periphery. The peripheral states export their primary resources—raw materials—to the dominant regions in exchange for manufactured goods. Part of the periphery consists of countries that border one of the dominant regions. Due to their geographical proximity, they are economically dependent on markets in the Northern Hemisphere. While forming a semi-integrated economic ensemble with their adjacent and wealthy neighbors to the north, they remain largely closed to the rest of the world.

Each sphere will continue to extract profits from its periphery, made up of a group of underdeveloped nations. The periphery of the Pacific sphere is infinitely more promising than that of the European sphere. It includes Burma, Thailand, Malaysia, Indonesia, the Philippines, and the countries of Latin America. The Asian countries, almost all future "tigers," are already growing rapidly—five times more rapidly than Africa. Their enormous demographic growth—there are already more young people in Indonesia than in all the European Community—is a plus, if (and it is a big if) the rate of economic growth keeps pace with population growth, making consumers out of the masses.

The countries of the Latin American periphery are in a much less promising position. Their indebtedness will stifle development, making the organization of an efficient market economy difficult. Their entrenched poverty will prevent democracy from sinking deep roots. Their dependence on raw-material exports will make it all but impossible to sustain growth. Already, several countries have embraced drugs—a pariah commodity—to sustain their wrecked national economies. An outlaw economic culture has become entrenched. A few countries, like Mexico (which is negotiating a historic free-trade agreement with the United States) and Venezuela, may be able to escape the vicious cycle of debt and poverty, thanks to oil. With considerable luck, they may be able to escape altogether the southern continent's slide into terminal poverty.

Europe's periphery, Africa, is a lost continent. It is one of the last places on earth in which famine persists. The terrible facts of having fallen into an economic black hole speak for themselves: since 1970, Africa's share of the world markets has been reduced by half; its debt has been multiplied by twenty and now equals its total gross product; income per capita in sub-Saharan Africa has fallen by one quarter since 1987. Africa's population growth has always outstripped its economic progress, making demographic expansion a handicap instead of an asset. The current population of 450 million will double in the next twenty years, when there will be more people in Nigeria alone than in the Soviet Union today. Falling exports and investments, coupled with aging machinery and equipment leftover from colonial rule, guarantees that the economic plight will only grow worse. The most probable future for Africa is tragic: it will be the only region on the whole planet that is entirely excluded from abundance. There is a single possible exception: with enormous luck and skill, South Africa may well emerge relatively unscathed from this fate.

For both Latin America and Africa, the fall in both the level of savings as well as investment, compounded by the debt burden, has accelerated a precipitous fall in the level of growth. Rising debt has proved particularly crushing. From 1978 to 1989, the debt in sub-Saharan Africa rose from $19 billion to $143 billion. In Latin America, during the same period, debt rose from $85 billion to $434 billion.

Three regions of the world remain largely outside the influence of tomorrow's dominant powers: the Middle East, India, and China, each with close to a billion people. Needless to say, if a miracle were to occur and they were to be fully integrated into the global economy and market, all strategic assumptions underpinning my prognostications would be overturned. That miracle is most unlikely.

The explosions that wrack the Middle East will echo far into the next century. The problems embodied in the North-South relationship converge in this region, and will continue to erupt into conflict. The region is volatile partly because there are no stable boundaries and the facts of national histories are still disputed by contending parties. In addition, as William Pfaff has rightly pointed out, the peoples of this region suffer from the terrible trauma of repeated defeats inflicted upon it by the West. These defeats have inspired both secular and religious fanaticism, characterized by paranoia and defiance, anxiety and frustration. But these movements of resistance are unlikely to produce models of development able to compete with the hyperindustrialism of the new world order. Of course, the accident of geological caprice, which has given five countries (Saudi Arabia, Iraq, Kuwait, Iran, and the United Arab Emirates) 60 percent of the world's known oil reserves, ensures that the question of who controls certain energy sources and who rules a given country will remain painfully important for a very long time to come.

India could experience particularly strong growth if it manages to sustain its opening to the world market. Many hundreds of millions of Indians could soon be active consumers. The subcontinent will become important to both the dominant regions of Europe and Japan, both of whom will try to bring it into their orbit as a beachhead for multinational companies and as an important strategic post for diplomacy.

China is engulfed in a long period of crisis and retreat as a result of the Tiananmen tragedy and the subsequent decision to pursue economic reform without political revision. This strategy will ultimately fail. As soon as the logic of market reform regains momentum, rapid political progress will be possible once again. Since it would not like to be crushed under the weight of economic refugees in the next century,

Japan has a keen interest in helping to develop the Chinese market.

Demography and its relentless logic will weigh heavily on the future of the planet. By 2050, 8 billion people will populate the earth. More than two thirds of the children born today will live in the twenty poorest countries. In thirty years, there will be 360 million more inhabitants in China, 600 million more in India, and 100 million more in Nigeria, Bangladesh, and Pakistan. The population of Nigeria, which doubles every twenty-two years, will equal today's world population in 140 years. By 2050, the number of people of working age in the world will have tripled. More than half of the global population will then be urban, as compared to one third today. Mexico City alone will have 30 million inhabitants before the end of the century. Across the world, 100 million children under five years of age will die of hunger or disease.

Seeking to escape from their desperate fate, millions will attempt to leave behind the misery of the periphery to seek a decent life elsewhere: they will become nomads of a different kind, a new version of the desert nomad migrating from place to place looking for a few drops of what we have in Los Angeles, Berlin, or Paris, which for them will be oases of hope, emerald cities of plenty and high-tech magic. Or, they will redefine hope in fundamentalist terms altogether outside modernity. This dynamic threatens true world war of a new type, of terrorism that can suddenly rip the vulnerable fabric of complex systems.

Latin American and Asian populations already press at the doors of the Pacific rim. In the United States (where the Hispanic population is 20 million and counting) migration will upset the cultural and linguistic balance, transforming the very nature of America, severing it from its Anglo-Saxon and European origins. It is possible, of course, that America will be able to absorb this shock and turn it to its advantage. After all, there is in the very idea of the country the sense that no one people or ethnic strain has a privileged purchase on the national identity or character. The notion of a melting pot is not without historical basis. The future of the United States lies in Latin America.

Europe is likely to have more trouble. The logic of continental integration confronts a long and bloody tradition of ethnic and national rivalries, a history of chauvinism and xenophobia. Mass migration from Africa, coupled with the flooding into the western and more prosperous states by hard-pressed Eastern Europeans, will prompt the construction of a new Berlin Wall—a wall that seeks to prevent the people of the periphery from seeking refuge in the centers of the prosperous North. The migration of these nomads will be regulated, since a rationalized and controlled flow of migrants will be advantageous. Much as Germany uses Turkish *Gastarbeiter* to do work few Germans are willing to do, so will the intermediary states of the emerging world order need workers from the periphery, for specific work for specific amounts of time. Many peripheral elites will continue to live, work, and travel in the privileged regions, enriching societies of the center with exotic music, images, cultures, and cuisines. But neither the Pacific nor European spheres will accept the majority of poor nomads. They will defend their cultural and political identity. They will close their borders to immigrants who refuse, after a decent interval, to return to their own benighted lands. Quotas will be erected and restrictions imposed for citizenship and for property. Social norms will ostracize foreigners. Like the fortified cities of the Middle Ages, the centers of privilege will construct barricades of all kinds, trying to protect their wealth and their internal stability. The failure of Marxism is seen in the Third World as the failure of Western culture and an end to the fight against systemic misery. This failure will inspire fanaticisms of all kinds.

The problem of borders could be resolved by the integration, over time, of the peripheral countries into their neighboring regions to the north. Following the pattern of Europe, for example, the United States, Mexico, and Canada are currently preparing to establish a free-trade zone stretching from Toronto to Tampico. One can imagine a similar arrangement between the intermediary states of the hinterland and the marginal nations of the periphery, thus opening up the possibility of enlarging democratic market-oriented zones in large regions across the world. Nevertheless, even if such North-South accommodation along borders were to occur, it would not solve the structural distress of the periphery as a whole.

THE REAL loser of the next millennium will be the planet itself if the imperative of the market is allowed to run rampant without constraint. Natural resources, which took billions of years to create, will be depleted as the earth is overrun by nomads loaded down with objects fabricated out of irreplaceable raw materials. If the current generation does not combat the compulsion to possess everything, all future generations will be losers.

The growing population of the planet calls for an even faster rate of economic growth to keep pace. Yet, given the state of current technology, this growth will cause more and more pollution, perhaps irreversibly ruining the environment that nourishes and sustains all life. The numbers are telling: since the beginning of the eighteenth century, while world population has grown by a factor of eight, production has increased one hundredfold. In just the past forty years alone, industrial production has multiplied by seven and the consumption of mineral resources has tripled. By the year 2000, it is estimated that world consumption of oil and coal will double. Due to cost and security and waste disposal problems, nuclear energy cannot, in the short term, substitute for oil. Neither can the still-underdeveloped potential of solar or wind power. Water is also becoming scarce. In the periphery, a fifth of city dwellers and three quarters of those in the countryside do not have adequate access to water. As a consequence, it is thought that 2 million to 3 million acres of cultivated land are being lost every year.

Runaway industrialism has introduced extremely noxious solid wastes and gaseous by-products into the environment. Solid wastes are piling up. Soon we will produce enough garbage annually to bury every urban area beneath a refuse layer one hundred meters thick. How will we get rid of this waste? Where will we put it? Will the periphery become one gigantic toxic dumping ground for the poisonous garbage of the privileged? The gaseous emissions spewed into the air by industrial production are another menace. The quantity of gases emitted over the past two centuries by the industrial societies, whether capitalist or Communist, are responsible for the warming of the atmosphere, the so-called greenhouse effect. We know the principal culprits: carbon dioxide, which is created through the burning of coal, oil, and natural gas; chlorofluorocarbons, which destroy the ozone in the stratosphere; methane, which is produced by farming and the breeding of livestock; and nitrogen oxide.

In the past century, the level of methane in the atmosphere has doubled and the level of carbon dioxide has grown by a fourth. Industrialized countries, which represent only 25 percent of the world's population, emit 75 percent of the greenhouse gases. According to the 1985 *Energy Statistics Yearbook,* issued under the auspices of the United Nations, the United States was responsible for nearly 26 percent of the carbon dioxide emissions generated by the major industrial countries; the Soviet Union was to blame for almost 18 percent, China for almost 10 percent, and Japan just over 5 percent. (Even though Japan's gross national product, some $1.2 trillion, was fully one third of the U.S. gross national product in 1986, Japan's carbon dioxide emissions were only one fifth of those of the United States.) Chlorofluorocarbons, of course, reduce the layer of ozone that surrounds the atmosphere, and are responsible for an increase in skin cancers. Carbon dioxide raises the temperature of the atmosphere. In the past one hundred years, the average temperature on the earth's surface has grown by half a degree. The 1980s were the hottest decade in a century. The polar caps have begun to melt and the level of the oceans is rising by two millimeters a year. Some computer simulations predict that the earth will heat up by more than two degrees centigrade before 2050 and that between now and the end of the next century the oceans will rise by at least half a meter, possibly by two meters. One can only imagine the catastrophic consequence of rising seas: seven of the ten largest cities in the world are ports, and one out of every three people in the world lives on a seacoast.

Sulfur and nitrogen oxides are destroying forests across the globe, particularly the fragile rainforests of the periphery, which are being devoured by the paper industry and agricultural expansion. Since the eighteenth century, an area the size of Europe has been denuded of its forests. In just ten years, half of the forest reserves of the western half of Germany have disappeared. In 1989, forest lands totaling an area larger than Switzerland and the Netherlands combined were erased from the world map. At this rate, an area eighteen times larger than this will have been devastated by the year 2000. Hyperindustrial Japan, currently the world's largest importer of tropical timber, already accounts for a third of the damage.

Deforestation is ruining the environment, which is the essential storehouse for the diverse heritage of the planet's plant and animal life. Close to 15,000 living species disappear each year, paralleling the daily death of languages and cultures that are overwhelmed by the flood of homogeneity that accompanies the triumphant market. All hope is not lost, however. In the privileged regions, this agonizing reality has already inspired ecologically sensitive movements that seek to reorient industrial policies. Countries of the North are controlling their birth rates. They are producing goods that require less energy but use more information, thus causing less pollution. In order to stabilize the concentrations of greenhouse-effect gases at their present levels, several European countries have committed themselves to reducing emissions into the atmosphere by at least 60 percent. Already, international accords are curtailing the worst offenders. Nitrogen oxide emissions in North America and Europe have fallen slightly in the past ten years, and chlorofluorocarbons will probably disappear altogether in fifteen years. Japanese industry has already attained a level of energy efficiency that is twice as efficient as the large European countries. Germany intends to stabilize emissions by the year 2005, and Sweden is ready to introduce a tax on carbon dioxide. The European Community is committed to preventing the increase of its carbon dioxide emissions.

Many in the North have proposed limiting economic growth in the South so that the earth's environment will be protected. The periphery has neither the financial nor the technological means to play by the new rules of industrial development. Despite the more stringent restrictions imposed on the developed industrial countries, carbon dioxide emissions per capita, to take only one example, will double globally by 2030, effectively nullifying the new eco-habits being adopted by the North. The peoples of the periphery will reject restrictions that would, in effect, safeguard the wealth and comforts the privileged North has gained over the past four centuries at the expense of the biosphere. Why should China or India, say, go without refrigerators so that affluent white-skinned Northerners won't get melanoma? Already Brazil refuses to renounce the burning of a parcel of

Amazonian forest unless the industrialized countries begin to substantially reduce their own carbon dioxide emissions.

IN A world turned upside down by nomadism, the need for a scapegoat will reappear. A half century after the end of the Second World War, the specter of racism again haunts a forgetful planet. The new racism will have many faces: it reveals itself in the opposition between Islam and Christianity, and it can already be seen in the widespread hostility to dark-skinned immigrants who search for home and hearth in the inhospitable North. If the people of power in the emerging spheres of prosperity knew how to think in the long term, they would watch carefully the peripheries at their doors. In the coming world order, there will be winners and there will be losers. The losers will outnumber the winners by an unimaginable factor. They will yearn for the chance to live decently, and they are likely to be denied that chance. They will encounter rampant prejudice and fear. They will find themselves penned in, asphyxiated by pollution, neglected through indifference. The horrors of the twentieth century will fade by comparison.

IV

Nomadic Man

UMANITY IS entering a hyperindustrial age. New zones of wealth will exist uneasily alongside vast regions of poverty. Advanced technologies will create a class of products and goods that will empower individuals as never before while shattering traditional bonds to country, community, and family. These new objects, which I call nomadic, because they are small and portable, will alter relationships across the spectrum of modern life. Above all, they will change man's relationship to himself.

These objects—whose embryonic forms, like the Sony Walkman or the laptop computer, are ubiquitous today—will help create a different human being. Men and women will no longer be the naked nomads of the earliest sacred order societies, wandering from well to well, searching for water to survive. Nor will they be the dangerous, hunted nomads of the order of force. Instead, the privileged residents of both the European and Pacific spheres, and of the richest regions of their peripheries, will be empowered, liberated nomads bound by nothing but desire and imagination, greed and ambition. This new nomadic elite is already forming, severing its ties with any particular place, whether nation or neighborhood.

PEOPLE HAVE always had nomadic objects, essential tools for human survival: stone and flint for making fire; amulets for warding off evil and disease; hammers and other tools for building shelter; weapons, from spears to guns, for defense and for war; coins and the letter of credit for the buying and selling of goods, to list only a few examples. These precious objects have often been a way of measuring the relative power of their possessor. Throughout history, the three orders of the sacred, of force, and of money have tended to imbue these objects with a special significance.

Today, as we enter the ninth market form, new nomadic objects are being created. Services of all kinds are being transformed into objects, their functions increasingly designed to be portable, to be nomadic. For example, the merchant has always dreamed of having objects light enough to transport easily and cheaply. Those objects that industry is creating now—and will invent more and more of tomorrow—

will be less and less heavy and bulky. They will be mobile, embodying knowledge, providing communication, executing a myriad of services by substituting for the people who perform such services today. These tiny machines, some no bigger than the width of three human hairs, are expected to have profound implications for industry in general and for health care in particular.

THE NOMADIC objects of the future will prompt new relationships with the city and the family, with life and death. Indeed, they will more radically transform life in the second millennium than the automobile and television changed the way of life of the twentieth century. These new goods will not spring full-blown from the fevered fantasies of nerds and techno-freaks, but from the competitive imperative of industry, always alert for ways to turn human desires and needs into profitable products. Socially irresistible, economically profitable, these new objects are already, to some degree, technically possible.

In order to describe the dawn of this new age, I must calculate as an astronomer figures the trajectory of a star whose existence is suspected but unconfirmed—by looking at the particular movement and characteristics of similar stars. By doing so we will be better able to understand the dynamic market forces that are impelling the invention of the nomadic objects of the future. We will see how the crisis of the eighth market form is itself a principal factor in their creation.

All previous market forms since the thirteenth century have withered for essentially the same reason: as the center (whether Antwerp or Amsterdam or London) tries to maintain its hold on the world economy, it invariably seeks to close the gap between the escalating cost of producing services and goods and declining profits by incurring more debt than can be repaid by newly created wealth. Excess debt always leads to inflation, bankruptcy, and financial collapse. Historically, in the wake of a crisis of debt, new technologies that make the manufacture of existing goods more efficient are introduced, thus reducing the relative cost of services needed for maintaining the market form.

This occurs when businesses are able to apply the new technology to services previously outside the market, thereby transforming them into commodities that can be mass-produced in a cost-efficient (that is to say, a profitable) way to meet social demand. The crisis ends with the reconstruction of a new market form organized around a different geographic center and a new consumer good. New technology is the engine of new wealth creation.

IN THE mid-1960s the cost of producing services began to spiral upward as the economy sought to satisfy the rising social demands of a generally prosperous consuming public.

The rise in energy prices only made the problem worse. It was not its chief cause. Three services—education, health care, and defense—were more culpable, for they began collectively to consume a disproportionate share of all value produced by the industrial countries. As a result, both profits and wages began to fall.

The boom in higher education that began in the 1950s, especially in the United States, partly in response to the anxiety touched off by the successful Soviet launch of Sputnik, saw the creation of great multiversities, such as the University of California. This vastly escalated budgets for education. In the 1960s, the birth of Medicare confirmed the right to health care for all and would come to exert enormous strains on the federal budget. (The American bill for health care now exceeds $600 billion a year.) At the same time, military costs continued to escalate with the Cold War arms buildup and the Vietnam War.

In the absence of liquidity to maintain their purchasing power, the American consumer turned to Visa and Master-Card while corporations piled up debt to expand without the necessary equity, or just to stay in business, or to fend off takeovers. By 1986, the results were clear: the average American's individual debt amounted to an unprecedented 66 percent of his income, while corporate debt totaled 57 percent of overall business revenues, according to Harvard's Benjamin Friedman.

The growing awareness that such debt (which also plagues Japan and Europe) could not possibly be paid prompted the financial chaos of the 1980s in the world's principal money markets. The collapse of the savings and loan industry in the United States by the late 1980s, as well as the weakening of its other major banking institutions, illustrates the historical pattern. As in the past, market forms stumble and fall because the spending required to maintain world preeminence costs more than the total wealth that can be generated. Growth in the provision of services, which the privileged denizens of the center come to expect, and even to demand, like those provided by doctors and teachers in the most rapidly growing health and education sectors of the American economy, far exceeds a corresponding growth in productivity in these areas. This contrasts with the manufacturing of products, where efficiency usually grows with the expansion of production as the cost per unit falls. Thus, in spite of all efforts to contain health costs in the United States, they rose in the past decade from 8 percent to 11 percent of GNP, while education costs grew in the same period from 3 percent to 6 percent of GNP. The lesson: growth of services historically always reduces the overall profitability of the economy and squeezes resources for industrial investment.

THE USUAL response of rich societies to declining profits is to push consumers into ever greater debt so that they can afford to purchase more goods than it was previously possible for them to use and to pay for. With the aid of advertising, especially through the medium of television, all kinds of previously unimaginable dreams and desires were awakened. Now every car had to have a stereo in it; every household had to have a videocassette recorder; every tape player had to be replaced by a compact disc player; every yuppie, a status category itself defined by the reigning ethos of consumption, had to have a $40,000 BMW. Everyone lived for today without any thought of tomorrow. Buy now, pay later was the slogan of the hour. Savings plummeted.

The growth of consumer debt, in turn, deepened the crisis by generating and sustaining the further growth of services to manage debt and handle the information on which credit is based. Banks of all kinds proliferated, as did consumer finance companies. More and more people found work in the service sector. The number of jobs grew, but the health of the economy worsened. The structural crisis was aggravated, and its resolution postponed. For economic history teaches that only through transforming services into products that can be mass-produced in industrial fashion will profits be generated and sustained.

For example, consider the greatest innovation of marine technology of the sixteenth and seventeenth centuries, the flyboat, an innovation that was largely responsible for Amsterdam's ascension to the center of the world economy in those years. First developed around 1590, the flyboat was cheaper to construct than previous ships of similar purpose. According to K. H. D. Haley's authoritative *The Dutch in the Seventeenth Century,* the Dutch were able to accomplish this feat because of "relatively large-scale and standardized production, with the aid of labor-saving machinery—cranes for handling heavy timber, and, most important, wind-driven sawmills." The flyboat needed a smaller crew and was much more economical to run. Haley writes: "A Dutch ship of 200 tons might therefore need only ten men, while an English ship of the same size might carry as many as thirty. If it is true, in addition, that wages were lower and provisioning cheaper, the combined effect was to allow the Dutch to offer freight rates a third to a half lower than those, for instance, of their English competitors in the seventeenth century." History is spackled with similar examples. Economic renewal occurs only with the introduction and mass application of new technologies capable of reducing the costs of social demand through substituting products for services.

THE TECHNOLOGY that will permit the ninth market form to emerge is the microchip. It has already paved the way for the industrialization of services in a vast array of areas from the automated teller to medical diagnostics. The microchip is a tiny square of silicon on which millions of bits of information, accessible at the speed of light, are placed. Today, up to

16 million characters can be etched on one chip; by the end of the century it will accommodate a billion. So-called teraflop supercomputers, based on a technique known as massively parallel processing, capable of calculating more than a trillion mathematical operations each second, will, according to *The New York Times,* "help scientists and engineers in areas like simulating the body's reaction to a new drug without the need for human subjects; mapping the human genetic structure to better understand inherited diseases; generating models of the world's climates to study changes induced by air pollutants, and recognizing spoken languages and images in order to improve the versatility of factory robots." Applied to the practical tasks of reducing the cost both of manufacturing and labor-intensive services, microchip-based machines will generate exponential economic growth with enormous profits, providing a vast sum for new investment.

The microchip—the modern counterpart to the flyboat, or the later steam engine, which multiplied the power of animal traction many times over—is the principal source of recent growth in productivity across the advanced industrial world. Robots programmed by microprocessors have reduced the cost of manufacturing such products as the automobile. According to Kenichi Ohmae, one of Japan's leading management analysts and author of *The Borderless World,* the nine Japanese auto companies employ just 600,000 workers to produce 12 million cars each year. By contrast, it takes

Detroit some 2.5 million workers to produce the same number.

The real growth in the twenty-first century will take place as services—first in communication and later in health and education—are transformed into products that, because they embody functions formerly provided by people, may be more properly called objects. *Object, machine, instrument, equipment*—it is difficult to choose a word that describes exactly this new industrial development. Aren't automobiles and televisions objects? More and more, thanks to the computer, the objects of the future will move, talk, and work. These are, then, more like machines, or instruments. If I don't use any of these appellations, it's because they refer to prior technologies based on the use of energy, not on the manipulation of information, which is, perhaps, the chief characteristic of the nomadic object of the future. More generically, the word *object* corresponds better to the nature of those things that remain, above all, products, no matter what their intended use is.

Like the objects of pagan antiquity, the nomadic objects of the future will not be inert, but will represent the life, mind, and values of those who create and use them. They will essentially be extensions of our senses and of our bodily functions. Computers extend the human brain, for instance, and are expected one day to offer a kind of artificial intelligence. New computerized teaching instruments, tantamount to placing the entire holdings of the Library of Congress or the British Museum at the disposal of every student, will replicate in individualized form the education once only provided in a standard manner by schools. The transistor, an essential innovation, first made radio (an example of an early industrial nomadic object) portable, and then made listening to music mobile. Later, the tape recorder, then the Sony Walkman, allowed the consumer, a traveler in space, to listen to music wherever he wanted, whenever he wanted. In the same way, the videotape recorder permits him to travel in time. Programmed by a quartz clock, another major innovation, the videotape recorder stores images that can be viewed at a later time. It replaces an expensive service (television broadcasts) by a private object (the cassette). The compact disc, as well as the videodisc, have allowed us to see, to hear, and to store in an extremely small space, sounds and images, to sell them in multiple copies, and to collect them. Finally, the communication of images, of forms, and of sounds is even more developed with synthesizers, multiple-screen televisions, and scanners.

More recently, the personal computer—a miniaturization of machines providing business computing—has replaced innumerable services previously performed for private persons by private persons: secretaries, researchers, accountants. It gives direct access to game programs (leisure and entertainment), to data bases of all kinds (education), or to exercise programs (health care). The individual consumer can use this remarkable object to resolve problems or obtain services. Special coded electromagnetic memory cards, such as automated teller cards, allow the consumer to pay for services and to store confidential information. It establishes a new relationship with money and forces a reorganization of the banking system.

COMMUNICATIONS for the modern nomad are becoming simpler and more convenient. Messages can be received from the telephone answering machine, which can even be consulted from far away. Thanks to the portable telephone, the nomad can continue to conduct his public and private life with others no matter where he happens to be, whether driving a car, strolling on a beach, flying in an airplane. There are no more excuses, there are no more sanctuaries, there is nowhere left to hide. There is, of course, a great irony in this development. Ostensibly liberating people from their ties to place, such nomadic objects make it harder than ever to escape from the world of work. It was once thought that a postscarcity, hyperindustrial world would enable people to reduce the time they spent working and increase their leisure activity. Just the opposite has occurred. Nomadic man will labor ceaselessly, because the natural divisions of day and night and of time itself will have been banished. The facsimile machine reduces the time it takes to communicate images, drawings, manuscripts, letters, and missives of all kinds, to the time of a telephone call. For the first time in history, man will not have an address. The sense of place that gave birth to all previous cultures will become little more than a vague regret.

The nomadic objects that have invaded our lives form a galaxy of goods—at first glance disordered, disconnected, incoherent. In reality, however, they are united by a single governing principle: they are designed to manipulate information—images, forms, sounds—at great speed, transforming services performed by people for other people into objects, at once portable and usable, produced by industrial processes. For example, the preparation and provision of food is an area in which time-dependent services already have become mass-produced objects. Freezing allows long-term storage of foodstuffs. Microwave ovens have transformed the preparation of meals. Now, instead of cooking, one can buy a prepackaged, mass-prepared meal, to be consumed either at home or at work, that can be ready to eat in minutes, even seconds. One eats whenever one wants to, wherever one is. Whether in a car, a plane, a train, a boat, or at home, one now eats while moving, so as not to lose time. Dishes that are quick to prepare, ready to cook and serve are in great demand.

IN JUST a few years, nomadic objects have proliferated, changing the daily lives both of those who can afford them and those who dream of possessing them. Their existence, however, has scarcely affected the economic travail of the eighth market form, for such objects have yet to significantly affect the two most critical sectors of the economy— education and health. Nevertheless, by priming the consumer to use them, and industry to produce them, nomadic objects in the food and communications sectors have paved the way for similar objects elsewhere.

But can such objects be invented? Will they really be able to replace the services performed by the doctor and the teacher? The answer would appear to be no. It seems impossible that man could be excluded from the act of healing, or from teaching others. But the process has already begun. The logic of the market pushes forward and the cultural ground is now being prepared.

Individuals everywhere in the privileged regions of the world are enrolling in the cult of the healthy and of the well informed. Standards of beauty, once so varied and different from society to society, are now increasingly blended into a single, homogenized ideal. An individual will want to protect his health, prolong life, and remain attractive by staying in physical shape through exercise and weight control. The market of those seeking to be in shape and informed is large and lucrative. The worldwide success of Jane Fonda's exercise regimen and Robert Fulghum's homilies testify to the broad appeal of these ideals. The constant injunctions to eat properly, stop smoking, cut fat intake, and so on are heard everywhere.

Citizens of the fast world, if they are to partake of its offerings, must work hard to win and maintain the right to their autonomy. To live to a ripe old age, to find work more easily, the citizen-consumer must monitor his health and mind his education. Advancing a career depends upon obtaining and maintaining a certain level of education. There is no future in unskilled labor. Machines are the new proletariat. The working class is being given its walking papers. Nomadic man is taught that if he is to find work more easily, he must not count too much on society to keep him in shape. He must regard himself as his own sculptor. Hence, the proliferation of health clubs, self-help books, and university extension courses.

The cultural ideal that these aspirations embody is that of the movie star, or model. What began in the arenas of popular music and fashion—the hit parade and trendy clothes—is now a social phenomenon that has gone global, refusing to respect class, ethnic, or national boundaries. Slowly and surely and seductively, the definition of the desirable has merged with that of the acceptable. Together they form a powerful and dangerous consensus, driving out what is deemed abnormal and ugly. The scapegoat is no longer simply he who has no money, but he who is not in good shape: the fat, the deformed, the lazy, the sick, the ignorant.

It is in response to the demand for uniformity of appearance that the critical nomadic technologies in health and education will emerge. For doctors and teachers have the social function of certifying that each person meets the standards society implicitly imposes on its members. Such objects, designed to monitor appearance and measure health, already exist. Some are used privately and are of distant origin, such as the mirror to judge one's beauty, the scale to watch one's weight, the thermometer to take one's temperature. Examples of nomadic objects of more recent vintage include self-tests for alcohol levels, fat content, even for pregnancy. Others must still be used by trained professionals: electrocardiographs and arterial pressure monitors, for example. But technology is fast robbing the health professional of a reason to exist.

Objects of self-diagnosis will become increasingly sophisticated. They will use microprocessors to measure a parameter, compare it against the normal value, and announce the result of the test. For some time to come, only doctors will be permitted to use these new objects. But they will be miniaturized, simplified, manufactured at a very low cost, and made available to all consumers, despite the strong opposition of the medical profession with whom they will compete. One day, everyone will wear a wrist instrument that will continuously record the beat of the heart, arterial pressure, and cholesterol level.

Even cancer treatment and surgery may one day be self-administered. Isemi Igarashi, executive vice president of Toyota's research department, envisions a microscopic capsule that could be launched on a cancer search-and-destroy mission in the bloodstream of an individual. Researchers are already perfecting a tiny biomedical sensor for measuring blood flow. So much promise is seen in the future of micromachines that in August 1990, Japan's Ministry of Industry and Trade chose such devices as the nation's next industrial target. Kenzo Inagaki, deputy director of the ministry's machinery division, believes that in the future "we could do surgery at home, saving the costs of hospitalization and surgery."

The desire to achieve mastery over oneself, to equip oneself with early warning systems able to detect the onslaught of disease or physical deterioration, the increasing familiarity with display screens and computer-generated images, the growing distrust of the medical establishment, combined with the faith in the technological superiority (even infallibility) of nomadic objects will open enormous markets for these devices. Medical practitioners, deprived of a portion of their traditional function, will nevertheless find new roles in healing illnesses that, were it not for nomadic objects, would previously have gone undetected. They will also be helpful in the production and experimentation in the use of these medical self-surveillance gadgets.

Self-diagnostic devices will help measure educational progress. Already computer tests and educational games are preparing the public for this eventuality. As binary games, requiring only a yes or no, these games may easily be put into a computer's memory, making it possible for children to use the personal computer to assess their knowledge. Existing programs now allow each student to check what he or she has learned, and to study for examinations at home in many different subjects, and at many levels.

Nomadic objects of the same sort, but immensely more sophisticated, will allow children to learn, by themselves, knowledge that today is provided by the world of schools and teachers. The difference between education and play will blur; modern pedagogy is already preparing for the arrival of this day. To learn is to live by proxy, to travel by images. Nomadic man will study at all ages, on screens and with images that one will manipulate by oneself, driven by the need to be informed, to be au courant with everything that is going on in the world, this ephemeral succession of tragedies and comedies. Videodiscs will contain entire dictionaries to consult. Tomorrow, children will listen to the computer-teacher just as today they use a calculator instead of memorizing the multiplication tables. The camcorder will become much more advanced. Today it is a tool for leisure, tomorrow it will be an instrument for the permanent recording of information. It will become a tool for the retrieval of data, especially when it is merged with the personal computer. Entire libraries will be preserved in these portable video computers. Nomadic man can then browse whenever he wishes.

All these objects will use magnetic or optical memories whose capacities will reach several thousand billion characters. We will regard them as indispensable just as today we cannot imagine how we survived in the world before the arrival of the copy machine and the fax. Such objects will sustain economic growth far into the future. Because they will empower us as never before, we will be free to live where we wish, with the portable tools we need to stay in touch with each other, detached from the factories and office buildings of the past.

I have not chosen the word *nomad* by chance. Not only does it seem to me to characterize the industrial objects to come, but it is also the key term that best describes the culture of consumption and life-style of the next millennium. For example, entertainment and leisure will be devoted to the ideal of travel; television already allows us to come and go all over the world, in space and in time, in reality and in fiction. Moreover, it allows us to travel without ever stirring from our comfortable armchairs at home. Thus, we can partake of the nomadic life through the medium of television, switching from channel to channel. Living life through electronic images, we travel and experience the world vicariously and safely. Thus, a television program is a particularly profitable product, and it will continue to be in great demand for many years to come.

At the same time, the desire actually to embark on voyages will stimulate unprecedented growth in tourism. A major form of economic development, tourism will require a ceaseless growth in hotels and transportation, of ports and airports, of trains and highways in the Pacific and European spheres, as well as in the picturesque, if dangerous, periphery. These conveniences will provide the traveler with all the comforts of home. Just as television viewers will travel while staying still, tourists will always be surrounded by reminders of home while traveling.

Those who will not have access to these nomadic objects and to these dreams of travel will travel through the recycled images of other people's trips. Or, what is worse, through the use of stimulants of all kinds, especially drugs and alcohol. Industrial expansion is, it must be conceded, based on the promotion of values (the culture of choice) that lead to their use. Drugs are the nomadic substances of the millennial losers, of the excluded and the discarded. They provide a means of internal migration, a kind of perverse escape from a world that offers none.

Automobiles, airplanes, trains, and boats (the means of transportation that made modern nomadic culture possible in the first place) will be the privileged places of accumulation of second- and third-generation nomadic objects (telephones, facsimile machines, televisions, videodisc players, computers, microwave ovens). Since such objects are artificial limbs making travel less onerous, they will speak and work as if they were living beings. They will use many sources of energy: solar, nuclear, hydrogen. Nomadic man will regard them as if they were the covered wagons favored by the Gypsies.

The wristwatch will be the perfect nomadic object, the primary symbol of prestige and utility, the essential accessory. It already has many functions other than telling time: it can contain telephone numbers, addresses, a calculator. It can measure humidity and atmospheric temperature. It can include an electronic calendar and store innumerable bits of personal information, identification papers, cultural preferences. It is the link to multiple exterior networks, as well as a medicine dispenser. It is also a coveted item of nomadic clothing, an artificial limb, an ornament, the jewelry of nomadic man. One day, when sound is digitized, it will obey voice commands.

The telephone will soon be reduced to the size of a memory card that can be inserted into a tiny portable device. Linked by radio to complex electronic networks, it will allow a person to connect himself to whomever he wishes, without allowing anyone to know where he is. It will no longer matter where one is from. It will be enough to identify the millennial nomad by a number or just by his name. Calling his name will be enough to talk to him or to write to him. Facsimile will soon be, in its turn, the size of a personal memory card, able to be inserted in any suitable device, to receive all mail in his name without giving his address, no matter where he is. The memory card will become the principal artificial limb of a person, at once an identity card, a checkbook, a telephone, and a fax machine—in sum, nomadic man's passport. It will be a kind of artificial self.

To use it will only require plugging it into the global electronic networks of information and commerce, the oases of the new nomads. These networks will be as easily accessible, homogeneous, and integrated as today's automated tellers whose services we use by simply inserting our bank cards into their slots. Such networks of the future will be located in banks, stores, all public places (at least in the most wealthy metropolitan areas). One day, commands will be given by simply speaking.

Middle-level nomads will stay in places that are impersonal, like the hotels that today ring airports throughout the world. Only the most fortunate rich nomads will have the means to become property owners in the large cities, which will be the magnetic poles for their brethren from all areas and regions of the globe. Cities will be fortified, dangerous places, the tangled heart of electronic networks, a cabled field of dreams.

Nomadic objects of self-surveillance will make it possible for man to worship at the altar of Narcissus. Each consumer object will appear to nomadic man as if it were an amulet of antiquity, designed to ward off death and prolong life. Just as there is no mirror without cosmetics, no self-diagnosis without tools for self-conditioning, so too will the nomadic objects of tomorrow meet the need of nomadic man to render himself perfect. Mass-produced industrial products will permit anyone, once they have measured their variation from the healthy, socially approved standard, to bring themselves back to "normal." Examples already abound: medicines that cause weight loss; implants that restore beauty; contact lenses that give the eyes a more desirable color; wigs that can cover baldness; condoms and pills to avoid pregnancy; pacemakers that regulate cardiac rhythms.

A considerable step will be taken when one can connect microprocessors to different organs of the body, so as to permanently monitor variations from norms and reestablish equilibrium. Already, one can automatically inject insulin into diabetics; soon, vitamins may be injected into babies. These microprocessors, at first made out of materials the body can tolerate and later out of biological materials, will supply medicine at regular intervals.

Semiprosthetic devices, semicopies of the organs they are designed to repair or to supply, will revolutionize the treatment of illness. For many years, industry has fabricated and sold artificial joints, fingers, lenses, bones, heart valves, legs, and teeth, as well as artificial speech and movement aids.

Tomorrow we will fabricate artificial lungs, kidneys, stomachs, and hearts. Perhaps one day even livers. Is it impossible to imagine the unimaginable? That even the human brain might eventually be artificially reproduced? After all, genetic engineers are devising methods to permit the human body to be stimulated to defend or repair itself by gene therapy, through the implantation of genetically altered cells. Current therapeutic products include a human growth hormone to be used to combat dwarfism.

At the end of this cultural mutation, one can imagine that man himself will become a nomadic object. Covered with artificial organs, he will become an artificial organ himself, to be bought and sold like any other object. Fantasy? Mere extrapolation of present tendencies? Let us examine the possibility more closely.

Living things have been bought and sold for a long time. Animals and vegetables are not only marketed, but recently all animal and plant species may also be patented. They can be produced and sold like any other product. A critical threshold was crossed the day a manufacturer was recognized as the legal owner of a living species. Dietary demands have already led to animal breeding and the invention of artificial production processes for plants, then to the manufacture of artificial plants themselves. To profit from this research, industry has demanded the right to protect its products through the use of patents. For the same reasons, patents have already been issued for unicellular organisms and recently for multicellular organisms.

Knowing that man himself is only a particularly complex organism, we cannot avoid the prospect that some people may hope one day to patent a human being. Humanity has already taken the first step down this nightmarish road. Today, many people would like to be able to decide to have only one child. Artificial insemination, or in vitro fertilization, originally developed to help sterile parents to have children, also allows one to have children without the use of a living mate. One can imagine that one day soon a woman might choose to stockpile some of her eggs so that she may have children at a later date, chosen by her, with the sperm of a known or unknown donor. One day, she will also be able to choose the sex of the child, which will disturb one of the major statistical equilibriums of human history.

One can envision a time when parents will be able to choose the characteristics of the children they want to have. In the beginning, of course, people will try to avoid having children who run the risk of hereditary diseases or deformities. Who will be able to say no to them? Doctors will try to measure these risks by analyzing genes. Today, it is already possible to detect the genetic foundations of cystic fibrosis and of Down's syndrome. To find these sorts of flaws, projects are attempting to map and decode the more than 100,000 genes that define humans. If successful, such research might lead to the establishment of a sort of genetic identity card for each individual. It is a great scientific challenge—one of the most difficult ever attempted. Who can oppose it?

As always, the dangerous path is a slippery slope. First, we will manipulate genes to reduce risks. Then we will progress from healing pathological cases to modifying the normal case. Establishing a genetic identity card will allow us, at the moment of fertilization, ab initio, to avoid having an embryo that threatens to suffer from a fault in the genetic program. Then, we will want to repair genetic mistakes. Finally, we will try to conceive ab initio a "normal" embryo.

In the distant future, one can imagine that man will learn to replicate a series of a model that he himself has defined. He will be sorely tempted at this point to purchase and consume his own doubles, copies as it were, of beloved people or specially created dream men and women, hybrids made up from donations of particular features, chosen to achieve particular objectives. Already fetuses are bought and sold, and the healthy livers of the dead are sold to the living. One day, everyone will be able to make inventories of himself or of others, search through the storehouse of organs, consume other men as objects, and wander in other bodies and other minds.

The result will be a kind of nomadic madness. Man will create himself just as he manufactures merchandise. The distinction between culture and barbarism, between life and death, will dissolve. Where will we find death? In the destruction of the last clone of oneself, or in the forgetfulness of others? And will we still be able to speak of life when man is thought of as only a product and an object?

All this will mark a momentous turning point. The culture of choice, wed to the logic of the market, will deliver the means for man to gain an unprecedented degree of personal autonomy. Possession of (or access to) nomadic objects will be regarded as a sign of liberty and power. For just as pagan man gained strength from the consumption of objects he regarded as containing the spirit of life, so too will millennial man have enabled himself to consume, in the market sense of the word, morsels of himself. He will have enrolled himself in what will amount to a cult of industrial cannibalism.

V

The Abandonment of Sovereignty and the Need for Limits

E LIVE in a world that is simultaneously shrinking and expanding, growing closer and farther apart. News of the toppling of tyrants or the suppressing of dissenters is instantaneously broadcast around the world. Vast sums of money are electronically transmitted in seconds. National borders are increasingly irrelevant. And yet globalism is by no means triumphant. Tribalisms of all kinds flourish. Irredentism abounds. Cries for "self-determination" mount in a world in which the very idea of sovereignty is made meaningless by the seemingly intractable planetary problems that now confront humanity.

Never has the world been more in thrall to the laws of money. Capitalism is unabashedly confident of its superiority. It animates the culture of choice whose political expression is democracy. Its munificent promise has inspired a consensus that cuts across all boundaries, whether national, racial, class, or religious. It drives the competition for economic advantage, and inspires industrial creativity. It rewards winners and punishes losers.

But capitalism's very success creates the conditions for failure. The coming world order will be fraught with danger: the ninth market form, no matter where its center is located, will replace living acts with dead artifacts; it will treat nature as merchandise and turn man himself into a mass-produced commodity. It will create a chasm between rich nomads and poor nomads. The dream of endless choice may end in a nightmare of no choice at all. A world of abundance may founder in an age of scarcity. The earth, after all, is not blessed with an inexhaustible stock of resources.

The next millennium will be terrible or magnificent, depending on our ability to limit our dreams. Not everything is possible, or should be. We must have the wisdom to curtail our dreams. There are limits (ethical and biological) that we transgress at our peril. To create a civilization that endures, humanity must somehow reconcile itself with nature and with itself. It must embrace a pluralistic and tolerant political culture that is imbued with a profound sense of the sacred.

Our survival as a species demands no less. The most pressing problem of the future will be the struggle to learn how to manage problems that are, for the first time, global in nature.

"Globality" characterizes the problems that confront us. Wealth and poverty, immigration and development, drugs, disarmament, and the environment are all inextricably linked. We will need to muster a new political vision and found new institutions that can compensate for the inherent limitations of the nation-state, and the constraining logic of the market. A vision of global stewardship will require, above all, political leaders who recognize the need for limits and have the courage to abandon traditional notions of national sovereignty. Such a course will doubtless face enormous obstacles. But such obstacles can hardly be greater than those surmounted by the newly emergent nation-states at the end of the eighteenth century. The transition from the age of monarchy to the era of rule by law and the separation of powers was to the men of that time as momentous and precarious a passage as the new millennium we are now entering.

Never before have people held as much power to shape their future as they do today. And never before have there been so many urgent decisions to be taken by a single generation in order for the world to realize its tremendous potential for prosperity while remaining livable. It would be foolhardy and even offensive if I were to assure my readers that these decisions will be made. Today, as in the past, many things are beyond prediction. Unexpected events, unlikely men and women, improbable ideas all burst forth when one least expects them. Individuals, whether Mohammed or Luther in the past or Gorbachev today, have the extraordinary ability to bend history in a direction and with a speed no astrologer, however prescient, or professor, however erudite, can possibly anticipate. All that can be reasonably said is that the world will change more in the next ten years than in any other period of history.

Nevertheless, as I have tried to suggest throughout these reflections, the dawn of the next millennium, in its force fields as well as in its diverse hazards, can be discerned in a general sense. This much is clear: between now and the year 2000, the order of money will become universal. From Santiago to Beijing, from Johannesburg to Moscow, all economic systems will worship at the altar of the market. People everywhere will sacrifice for the gods of profit. Two economic spheres—competing, unstable, but increasingly homogeneous—will struggle for supremacy, one organized around the Pacific, the other around Europe. They will compete for minds, methods, and markets. In each of them, military prowess will give way to economic might. Democracy will generally hold sway.

This evolution is not certain. In the Pacific sphere, for example, America will eventually react to Japanese power. This will occur when its dependence becomes painfully (and embarrassingly) evident. The United States is then likely to turn in upon itself, creating massive programs to catch up, establishing an industrial policy by increasing the government's intervention in the economy, particularly in financial services. Doubtless it will turn toward Latin America and Europe to find support and market outlets. If events confirm the end of the Cold War, America will have been relieved of the military burden of defending the continent from Soviet expansionism. This may make it possible for Americans to gradually find a sort of economic, political, and financial equilibrium.

The success of this belated effort is not at all certain, unless Americans are willing to accept a lasting shift from consumption to savings, something that would be politically unpalatable for those with the courage to urge such policies of reform and reconstruction.

In the European sphere, a harmonious integration of the continent is not at all sure. There are many obstacles to be overcome before the tendency toward economic union finds its political expression. But it will one day happen, if only because without progress in this direction all other gains will have been placed in jeopardy. For example, if the creation of a monetary union does not rapidly lead to the creation of a central bank, and to a common currency, the free circulation of men, of capital, and of goods will have been made untenable. Moreover, if all-European institutions are not democratized and their membership opened to all countries in the region, then decisions that affect all the nations of Europe will become impossible for all to respect. The present twelve members of the European Community have too much to lose by retreating not to advance in this direction.

In the eastern half of the European sphere, the delirium of newly acquired freedom has already given way to pessimism, if not outright despair. Economies are fragile, people impatient. Prosperity eludes them while bitterness deepens. The virus of totalitarianism is not fully expunged, and, as ever, it is harder to govern than it is to oppose. The reappearance of authoritarian regimes cannot be excluded. Even the breakup of some nations can be expected. The rage to settle accounts will inflame passions that refuse to be stilled. Nevertheless, I believe that reason is likely to prevail and that Europeans will not make the same mistake three times in one century. Is this too optimistic? Perhaps. I would be less than honest if I did not confess to harboring fears. No matter. The dice have been rolled, and nothing and no one can pretend that they have not been played.

If all goes smoothly in the two contending spheres, years of economic expansion lie ahead. Nomadic objects will underpin the hyperindustrialism of both spheres. They will fundamentally alter the relationships between people and their health, education, culture, and communication; they will transform the organization of work, transportation, leisure, the city, and the family. They will become the means of creation and destruction, of subversion and unification, of democracy and revolution. The winners of this new era will be creators, and it is to them that power and wealth will flow. The need to shape, to invent, to create will blur the border between production and consumption. Creation will not be a form of consumption anymore, but will become work—work that will be handsomely rewarded. The child who learns, the adult who guards his health, the creator who turns dreams into objects will be considered as workers who deserve prestige and society's gratitude and remuneration.

At the speed with which things change, none of this may seem inevitable today. When everyone understands that the major challenges of the twenty-first century are global, that the immigration problem will combine with that of development, that the drug problem and the disarmament problem only have solutions on a world scale, that economic production that continues to grow in its present form threatens the survival of the human species, supporting more and more nomads, each of whom avidly wants more and more objects, each creating more and more trash—when everyone understands this, it may well be too late.

The challenges pushing us most urgently are the related issues of demographic explosion, poverty and drugs, the threat to the environment, genetic manipulation, and arms proliferation. We are far from fully understanding the implications of these problems. Solving them will require leaders who are prepared to accept an unpopular abandonment of sovereignty. People must protect themselves from themselves, stop thinking of themselves as the proprietors of the world and of the species, and recognize at last that man is only a tenant. Notions of sanctuary and stewardship and the sacred must become the slogans that underpin a global program of survival. Accomplishing this will require that we resist the perverse logic of the culture of choice. Leszek Kolakowski has written of the grave peril that humanity risks when it abandons the sacred: "Culture, when it loses its sacred sense, loses all sense. With the disappearance of the sacred, which imposed limits to the perfection that could be attained by the profane, arises one of the most dangerous illusions of our civilization—the illusion that there are no limits to the changes that human life can undergo, that society is 'in principle' an endlessly flexible thing, and that to deny this flexibility and this perfectability is to deny man's total autonomy and thus to deny man himself. . . . The utopia of man's perfect autonomy and the hope of unlimited perfection may be the most efficient instruments of suicide ever to have been invented by human culture. To reject the sacred is to reject our own limits. It is also to reject the idea of evil."

The problems that will plague millennial man require that we restore the idea of evil, the idea of the sacred, to the center of political life. We must define world standards in a democratic way so that they may evolve in a manner that people everywhere will find acceptable. The institutions of the

United Nations were not designed for this mission. They have neither the means nor the mandate. They must move to a higher level of international organization by becoming institutions with a truly supernational authority, a genuine planetary political power that can impose standards in the areas in which the survival of the human species is at stake.

Few countries will easily accept such a transfer of power. I do not underestimate the difficulty of gaining the democratic adherence of such a scheme in a world of 7 or 8 billion people (with 5 billion below the level of survival). In its embryonic form, a regular summit meeting of heads of state representing the nations of the different continents may foreshadow such institutions and clarify some of the needed standards. If not, they will be imposed by committees of self-appointed experts or by obscure cabals.

International authority and institutions seem indispensable in at least five crucial areas: malnutrition, toxic gases, genetic engineering, armaments, and drugs. Saving children from sickness and ignorance requires the establishment of international finance organizations that devise new forms of donations and aid. Saving the environment requires a world agency to assess damage already done, such as to the ozone layer, and to establish standards of maximum allowable pollution, to measure deviations from such standards, and to aid poor countries in gaining access to technologies that will curtail and eventually eliminate pollutants of all kinds. Protecting the human species requires the establishment of universal standards that will allow us to control medically aided procreation, prenatal diagnostics, and genetic imprinting. We must agree upon the inviolability of the human body and of the individual and upon respect for individual privacy. The structures of life—the embryo as well as the gene—must be declared to be the inalienable property of the entire species and be given an absolute sanctuary free from manipulation, even if doing so will mean refusing to care for or to correct a genetic defect. We must be vigilant in order to avoid any actions in any country that might cause irreversible genetic mutation.

Protecting ourselves from worldwide arms proliferation will require the formation of a higher authority with democratically constituted powers. Such an authority will supersede bilateral negotiations, establish inventories, verify the application of agreements, and provide sanctions for violations, as much for chemical and biological and nuclear weapons as for more traditional arms. Protecting ourselves from the scourge of drugs will require international regulations aimed at excluding from the international financial community any institution that allows drug money to be laundered. In addition, an international agency must provide support to those countries that need to convert economies that depend on drugs, and to their struggle against narcotics profiteers.

It is not simple to imagine planetary institutions that are

simultaneously efficient and democratic, particularly in these complicated and contentious areas. Existing international bodies demonstrate how quickly bureaucracy blunts the ability to carry out such grand objectives. Still, humanity would be remiss if it did not make the attempt.

Nation-states will not disappear, of course. Even as the world becomes increasingly unified, even as technology and communications become universal and multinational corporations establish subsidiaries in every country, governmental power will remain largely local. This will be all to the good. Only states, inside historically stable frontiers, can assure democracy at the human scale. National governments will be assured of power in at least three areas:

Those countries closest to the center of the dominant sphere, whether Pacific or European, must place priority on attracting investment that will create jobs, industries, and services, and that will stimulate and sustain consumer demand. They will be responsible for obtaining or ensuring the creation of technologies that automate production, as well as store and process information. National governments will be responsible for building the network of communications—ports, trains, cities, fiber-optic networks, financial markets—so that they can attract other elements necessary to consolidate a center. The fate of whole countries will rest on the location of an airport, the laying of tracks for high-speed trains, the siting of industries dedicated to the manufacture and distribution of cultural images and products. Public budgets must be the principal means of financing these networks of prosperity. Some nations, of course, will have more market involvement in the mix, others less. But all countries that wish to succeed will need to welcome change, to make creation a fundamental ambition, invention a requirement, innovation a necessity. New ideas must be allowed to flourish and novelty must be rewarded.

The second task of national governments will be to ensure access to the new nomadic objects that will deliver health, knowledge, and culture. If access to the new technologies is assured to all individuals, they will have the means to blossom culturally and economically. The future of all countries will depend on their ability in these respects to redistribute resources so that each person can gain a share of the new hyperindustrial world. New ways of doing things will become necessary. Just as Social Security and family assistance allowed women to become consumers, so too must the consumers of nomadic objects—from the young to the old—have some minimal income. Allowances and student salaries will become institutionalized and decisively important: for a country, everything will depend on its ability to educate its citizens.

Finally, nation-states will differ according to the social project that they implicitly offer to their people. For some nations, each citizen must have the right to human dignity.

THE ABANDONMENT OF SOVEREIGNTY

For some, it will be enough to allow each person the right to become rich. For others, it will be the right to a decent income, to housing, and to some power in the workplace. Each nation will search in its own way and according to its own traditions for a new equilibrium between order and disorder, between plenitude and poverty, between dignity and humiliation.

ABOVE ALL, a new sacred covenant must be struck between man and nature so that the earth endures, so that the ephemeral gives way to the eternal, so that diversity resists homogeneity. Dignity must be supported over power and creativity must substitute for violence. In this new spirit, the wisdom of humanity—and not just the intelligence of machines—must be developed. Each person must have the means to invent a destiny. No one should be reduced to a spectator watching his own consumption. Individuals should be empowered to contribute to the heritage of civilization by giving it direction through the exercise of their liberty, aspiring to make of their own lives a work of art instead of a dull reproduction.

Can such a future be achieved through tolerance or exclusion? Through fanaticism or compassion? Immense uncertainty awaits us.

The ultimate answer to these perplexing questions is as always buried in words, for language is the key to wisdom.

The word *nomad* comes from an ancient Greek word that sought to express the notion "to divide," or "to split up into shares." Over time other meanings were attached to the word, one signifying "law" and another signifying "order." What does this linguistic evolution suggest?

That the nomad could survive only if he knew how to share his pastures with fellow men.

That without law there is no nomad. That the first nomadic object was law itself, which permitted man to organize the violence that threatened his existence and to live in peace.

That the Word received by Moses in the desert, in the form of stone tablets carried into the Tabernacle, still remains the most precious nomadic object in history because it is the Law that protects life and safeguards the sacred. That the nomadic object that we must protect above all others is the earth itself, that precious corner of the universe where life is miraculously perched.

The earth is like a library, to be left intact after enriching ourselves by reading it and after having been enriched by new authors. Life is the most precious book. We must handle it with love, careful not to tear any of its pages, in order that we may pass it on—with new commentaries—to others who will know how to decipher the language of their forebears in the hope of honoring the world they will leave to their sons and daughters.

JACQUES ATTALI was born in Algiers in 1943. A novelist, essayist, and writer, he has been special adviser to President Francois Mitterrand since 1981. A former professor of economics at the École Polytechnique in Paris, Attali is currently president of the European Bank for Reconstruction and Development in London.